study
guide

jennifer
strickland

beautiful
Lies

HARVEST HOUSE PUBLISHERS
EUGENE, OREGON

Cover by Left Coast Design, Portland, Oregon

Published in association with the literary agency of WordServe Literary Group, Ltd., 10152 S. Knoll Circle, Highlands Ranch, CO 80130

Cover illustration © Shutterstock / jumpingsack

Backcover author photo by Natasha Brown Photography (www.natashabrownphoto.com).

For the beautiful women
who have so bravely handed me a microphone,
granting me a voice in this generation:
You know who you are. This is written in your honor.

BEAUTIFUL LIES STUDY GUIDE
Copyright © 2013 by Jennifer Strickland
Published by Harvest House Publishers
Eugene, Oregon 97402
www.harvesthousepublishers.com

ISBN 978-0-7369-5626-0 (pbk.)
ISBN 978-0-7369-5627-7 (eBook)

Printed in the United States of America

13 14 15 16 17 18 19 20 21 / BP-JH / 10 9 8 7 6 5 4 3 2 1

Contents

A Letter from Jen

Dear Girlfriend,

If you are drawn to this message, I adore you already. The core of *Beautiful Lies* is based on one premise: We are more alike than we are different. We grapple with the same lies and need the same truths to free us.

About seven years ago, at the start of our ministry, the Lord began to etch this message on my heart. Today, my stack of Bibles and their falling-out, worn pages are tattered messes of highlights and scribbles which showcase truth after truth, like precious stones paving the pathway of the journey you are about to take.

This study is designed to help us see how the world imprints its darkest lies on our hearts, thereby twisting our vision of ourselves, others, and God. Conversely, this study helps us take a close look at the power born in us when we turn away from what we can see to what we can't see. When we look to God for our strength, value, and dignity, he is like a streaming light through the stained glass windows of our soul, illuminating the colorful picture of who he designed us to be.

My friend, I wrote this study because it was the one I needed; it is a journey I had to take to walk tall, strong, and whole. More than anything, I desire to be a better reflection of our beautiful God, to stop looking to temporary things to validate or define me, and to make a positive imprint on this war-torn, tumultuous world.

In this study, we will follow the book *Beautiful Lies*. We look at five lies of the world and five truths of the Word. The lies are effective because they are dressed attractively. On the surface, they look good. But we will look at what a roller-coaster ride it is when these five outside sources—men, mirrors, magazines, masks, and the media—control the way we see ourselves. I know the roller coaster. I've lived it.

These pages contain a journey I took because I needed it, but the truth is, I would never have taken it only for myself. It is written for you, and for your daughter, and for her daughter when her time comes. Because I believe we are the same. I believe at the finish line of this journey, you and I will be stronger, brighter, more purposeful, and more powerful than ever.

Let's walk this road together, remembering two are better than one, for two have an increased return on their investment. I know your precious time in these pages is an investment of your heart. I thank you for allowing me this special season of your life—to pour out my heart; to help you pour out yours, and then to stand back and be awed by the beauty.

You are cherished.

Jen

Introduction

Welcome to the *Beautiful Lies Study Guide*. While the book *Beautiful Lies* is written for every woman, the study is for a select group of women who want to delve deeper into their identity, value, and assignment as revealed by the Word. There is nothing more powerful than Bible study to give a woman deep convictions about who she is, who God is, and what she is here for. Founding your life on the Word instead of the world will make you a formidable force in the world.

This study is your journey: your pathway to discovering more deeply who God is, and in light of that, who you are and what your impact in the world will look like. There are options for you as you proceed. You can kick up your feet and read all of *Beautiful Lies* first and then review the chapters as you do the study, or you can read the book a chapter at a time and complete the study guide as you go. The important thing is to enjoy it! It matters more to me that you laughed or cried or opened your heart to God than that you just "filled in the blanks." The goal is to meet God in a new way, to see yourself as he sees you, and to share your journey, when appropriate, with your husband, friends, or daughters. The goal isn't just to "do a Bible study," but to relish his Word.

My suggestion, however, is to not take this journey alone. Partner with a friend, a group of friends, or your whole church; do it with other women. The accountability, friendship, and harmony of women's voices sharing their testimonies and truths holds tremendous power. As you meet with your group, decide on the pace that feels best to you. Take your time with the voyage. Don't feel rushed to complete any one section; instead, apply the Word and probing questions like a salve to the areas of your life which need it most. Soak in all the truths contained herein and go as deep and long and wide as the Spirit leads you. At the same time, however, make a goal to *finish*—and finish well. I would never have completed the writing of this study if I didn't have a date when it needed to be finished. So set the date of your finish line and keep it in mind as you run your race.

As you journey, be in prayer. Prayer and praise are our strongest weapons against the enemy. When trials and distractions come, don't be fooled! The enemy wants to stop you in your tracks, because if you finish well, equipped and ready for battle, you will be a force to be reckoned with! The enemy wants to steal your treasure, your joy, your inheritance, your purpose, your family, and your influence. Don't let him!

Be aware that you will be tested on the subjects we are studying; plan on it! I have been tested on all of it, and by no means do I think my period of testing is over! So be purposeful, returning regularly to your set-apart time with God in prayer, praise, and the Word. The more deeply rooted you are in him, the stronger your core will be.

During each of the ten weeks of our study, we will follow an infused pattern. On Day One, you will read a chapter of the book *Beautiful Lies* and answer some questions about it in your Study Guide. On Days Two, Three, and Four, you will study what the Word says about the topic of that week. Many of the weeks also include a "field trip," usually on Day Four. On that day, you will plan to get out of the house, sometimes by yourself and other times with a friend. So look ahead at the week's activities so you can plan accordingly. Regularly stepping away from the Word and engaging in the world is often the best way to define the world's lies and compare them to the truths we are embracing. On Day Five, you will meet with your group, watch a short video message from my website, and review the week's study together. Each day of our study, I have highlighted a "jewel for your journey." These are precious verses that lay out our pathway, Scriptures that I treasure, and I hope you will too.

As we journey, we will be looking at five "beautiful lies" and how allowing those lies to reflect our value can distort our God-given identities. Conversely, we will turn to the "gorgeous truth," the Word, where God clarifies for us what we look like in his eyes. Reclaiming our God-given identities is eye-opening, yet it is only the beginning. The real power comes for all of us when we realize how to live out our identity in our day-to-day lives. So take the time to answer the heart-probing questions along the way—they are there to help you walk out the destiny God has in mind for you.

May your journey through these truths be blessed and may you forever remember who you are and what you are worth…in his eyes.

Week 1 The First Lie:

You Are What Man Thinks of You

Day One: The First Lie

— Jewel for Your Journey —

"LORD, what are human beings that you care for them, mere mortals that you think of them? They are like a breath; their days are like a fleeting shadow" (Psalm 144:3-4).

Read the introduction and chapter 1. Use this space to journal your response. What did this chapter stir up in you? How did it make you feel? What or who did it make you think of and why?

Day Two: Defined

— Jewel for Your Journey —

"Do you see this woman?...I tell you, her many sins have been forgiven—as her great love has shown" (Luke 7:44,47).

I'm excited today to dig into the Word, because the Word always puts our life into perspective. We are going to start our study today by taking a look at the woman of Luke 7. This woman is nameless—the only name the Word gives her is "a woman...who lived a sinful life." I can imagine myself slipping right into her tattered dress and doing exactly what she does. I bet you can imagine yourself in her place too.

* Read Luke 7:36-50 and describe this woman's actions.

* What do you think her actions are expressing?

* Describe the Pharisee's response to her.

* Describe Jesus's response to her.

Jesus is obviously more endeared by the humble, contrite woman than he is with the prideful Pharisee. Everything she does lacks etiquette. My guess is her mascara is a mess. Her hair, which she uses as a mop for his feet, is dirty and infused with oil from the perfume. As she kisses his feet, her lipstick must be smeared, and as she cries, she can't possibly match the outward righteousness of those surrounding her.

Despite the Pharisee's rude thoughts, Jesus is very kind to him. Instead of rebuking him outright, Jesus teaches him a lesson couched in a parable. The story about the debtors illustrates that none of us can make up for our own sin: "There is no difference... for all have sinned and fall short of the glory of God, and all are justified freely by his grace through the redemption that came by Christ Jesus" (Romans 3:22-24).

Forgiveness is free, and the more lavish the forgiveness, the greater the gratitude.

Jesus follows the parable with a probing question for the Pharisee: "Now which of them will love him more?" What do you think is Jesus's highest value, as expressed in this passage? Circle one:

Faith   Repentance   Love   Forgiveness

* Leave a bookmark in Luke 7 and read 1 John 4:7-12. Fill in the blank: God is _____.

* How does John define love in verse 10?

* How does Jesus's treatment of the sinful woman match up with this passage of Scripture from 1 John?

* How does this passage convict the attitude of the Pharisee?

The Pharisee responds in judgment instead of love. I don't know about you, but I can jump into the robe of the Pharisee just as easily as I can wear the dress of the sinful woman. Somehow, the longer we are Christians, the easier it is to forget that we first came crawling to Jesus's feet in utter desperation. At least I did. When I came to Christ, I was broken and shamed, a living mess. I had made a mess of my life, and I carried such emotional wounds that I couldn't possibly hide them from God. And since that day, I have come before him broken and longing more times than I care to count.

Yet something insidious can happen to us. Instead of granting others the kind of grace we received, we can easily narrow our eyes at their frailty, their impropriety, their utter lack of etiquette in light of our perceived greatness.

* In what way do you see yourself in the Pharisee in this passage?

* What would happen if you jumped out of the Pharisee's rigid robe and into the soft tunic of Jesus? How would you look at and treat others differently?

Keep reading 1 John 4:13-19. These verses give me hope. They say that the love Jesus had for the sinful woman is the love that lives in us. We can love as Jesus did. And if we can love like that, people won't fear rejection from us. Perfect love creates an atmosphere of acceptance, and people are not afraid to be themselves in the presence of this kind of love.

* How does verse 18 define the essence of the interaction between the sinful woman and Jesus?

Turn back to Luke 7 now. The Pharisee labeled the woman a sinner. An evildoer. A wrongdoer. I can't tell you how many times in my life I've felt those words describe me. I seem to always mess up. But in Jesus's eyes, our actions, our past, and other people's labels don't define us. He does.

* What words does Jesus use to define the woman? Circle three:

Forgiven   Loved   Saved   Sinful

You got that right, sister! Jesus defines the woman by her love for him and his love for her. Her sin does not define her.

* What would be the result in this woman's life if she allowed Jesus's definition of her to be her identity?

* What would be the result in this woman's life if she allowed the Pharisee's definition of her to be her identity?

One of the biggest mistakes I made in my life was believing the first lie: "You are what man thinks of you." I wouldn't be surprised if this was the very lie that led the sinful woman to fall at Jesus's feet in the first place. Yet even when we are seeking forgiveness, even when we are pursuing a life of faith, even when we are pursuing God with all our hearts, people can try to define us in ways that are out of sync with Christ's definition of us.

Before we close today's lesson, I want you to think about some incorrect definitions people—or even the enemy—have assigned to you. I remember hearing words spoken by men that made me feel stupid, worthless, and unlovable. In fact, those were the words that led me to weep at Jesus's feet. I hear words like "failure" in my mind. No one has to speak them to me; I'm guilty of speaking them to myself.

* What about you? What incorrect definition have people (or even yourself) spoken over you that have impacted you negatively? How have those words affected you?

* Just as the sinful woman has a choice which voice to listen to, so do we. As we close today's study, use the space below to put yourself in the place of the woman falling unabashedly at Jesus's feet. Pour out your heart to him and listen closely for his words spoken back to you, writing them down here:

My friend, plant his words in your heart like seeds in fertile soil. Allow his view of you to grow. Like a vine of fragrant flowers, the way he sees you can change who you are, how you walk, how you look at others, and even the words you say to yourself.

* You are forgiven. Loved. Saved. Add other words God has added just for you:

Day Three: The Mirror of Man

—Jewel for Your Journey—

"God is not a man, so he does not lie. He is not human, so he does not change his mind" (Numbers 23:19 NLT).

It is quite appropriate that we started our study together by taking an up-close look at a messy woman. You are reading a study written by such a woman. In fact, I so identify with the sinful woman that one time I introduced myself as her to a crowd of proper Southern women. I had just moved from California to Texas when I was invited to speak at a famous Baptist church in Dallas. Showing up at the church, I could hardly believe the wealth—the facility alone rivaled the finest university in my mind! Looking out at the large crowd of well-dressed women who had just finished their delectable luncheon, I spoke into the microphone as I walked up on the stage: "Well, the sinful woman just came to your church. I hope she'll find acceptance here!" I believe this may have caught the women off guard, and anyone secretly wearing a Pharisee's robe had no choice but to shed it in an instant—after all, they were in church! Judgment's not allowed! The good news is, they accepted, embraced, and loved me—and I felt the same for them.

I still don't know how it is people invite me to speak on their stage; I always marvel at how I got there. Maybe it's their fascination with the modeling world. Maybe it's the romance of my story—of how God met me in faraway places, through unlikely people. Or maybe, just maybe, it's my unashamed poured-out passion for Jesus.

The woman who lived a sinful life was an emotional wreck, but she was also fantastically in love with Jesus—and he *so* loved her back. I believe the words he spoke to her—"Your faith has saved you; go in peace"—were foundational stones upon which she based her future steps.

When God planted salvation, forgiveness, and love in my heart, I was still living in Europe, modeling. I felt him telling me to "go in peace," and I did. Without hesitation I walked away from a lifetime invested in modeling because I longed to live free of man's demands. I wanted to be accepted in all my frailty, all my imperfection, and to find a destiny based on how I looked in his eyes and none other.

But man had planted lots of poisonous seeds in my heart, and they had taken deep roots I knew nothing about back then. Eventually, the poison ivy would be uprooted.

Over the course of the next two days, you and I will study man and his influence upon us. The Word makes some profound statements about men—meaning human beings, women included—and their lack of power to make us or break us. Don't mistake me: These are not "man-hating" verses. They are truth to set us free, meant to honor both God's and man's rightful place in our lives.

* Let's begin by looking at God and the comparison he draws between himself and man. Turn to Numbers 23:19, and write it here:

* What distinctions does God make between himself and man here?

* Now turn to Malachi 3:6 and write the first sentence here:

I love the simplicity of God. He states things so clearly: "I am not a man." "I do not change." "I do not lie." "I keep my promises." You don't get any simpler than that. Man, on the other hand, might change his mind—girl, I've been known to change my mind! I can flip-flop back and forth on something for longer than is healthy. I might even promise something and not deliver. I am fallen, imperfect, human, and fallible. In this verse, God is making that very point. He is not like man. Man might make an oath and then break it, a covenant and cancel it. Man might lie. God, however, never breaks his oath and cannot lie (Hebrews 6:18). He is faithful forever; he is the same forever. And here's the kicker: he doesn't change his mind about you. In a world that is constantly changing, this is one of my greatest comforts. I know God's not going to change his mind about me or about my destiny no matter how many times I fall. He might correct me in something, he might even rebuke me or severely discipline me, but he's not going to withdraw his love for me.

* Deuteronomy 31:8 says the Lord will "never leave you nor forsake you." What do these words mean to you personally?

The Beautiful Lie we are looking at this week is "You are what man thinks of you." In other words, man holds your destiny. Man reflects your beauty, value, and purpose. On the surface, we may not even know we have believed this lie. But beneath the surface, allowing man to be our mirror can poison our hearts and minds. Whether we are praised by men or insulted by them, we are not defined by what humans do or don't do, think or don't think, and say or don't say about us.

Let's take a look at a series of verses that answer the question "What is man?" for us.

First, turn to Psalm 144 and read verses 3-4. The Bible asks the simplest questions and gives us the clearest answers. Here, the Word asks the question, "What is man?" The answer likens man to a "breath." Other versions call man "a puff of air," "a passing shadow." (MSG, NKJV).

* Leave your bookmark in Psalm 144 because we will be coming back to it. Turn to James 4:14. What does James say about man here?

James so poignantly drives the point home by putting things in the second person: "You are a mist that appears for a little while and then vanishes." No doubt James was familiar with Psalm 144 as well as Isaiah 40:6-8:

> All people are like grass, and all their faithfulness is like the flowers of the field. The grass withers and the flowers fall, because the breath of the LORD blows on them. Surely the people are grass. The grass withers and the flowers fall, but the word of our God endures forever.

So not only are we but a breath, but we are also grass. We have our time of growth and beauty, but all God has to do is blow his breath on us and we are gone. The apostle Peter quoted these verses in 1 Peter 1:24-25. My guess is guys like James and Peter had to keep in mind that man didn't have the final verdict in their lives. As apostles after Jesus's death, burial, and resurrection, they dealt with continual opposition from men, and I'm sure they had to remind themselves often that men and their opinions about them were not mirrors. The only mirror they had to fix their gaze on was Jesus.

＊ Read Isaiah 2:22. What argument is God making here against putting your hope in man? Circle your answer:

Man is evil   Man is impermanent   Man is a liar

＊ Turn back now to the Psalms and read 146:3-6. What is the psalmist saying about putting your trust in man?

＊ What is the psalmist saying about putting your hope in God?

Both Genesis 3:19 and Ecclesiastes 3:20 say that man came from dust and to dust he shall return. But we know that God is forever.

＊ Turn now to some powerful words of Scripture, in Jeremiah 17:5-6. Describe the state of one who depends on man for his strength.

＊ Have you ever felt like you have depended on man for your strength, identity, and worth? Circle your answer:

Yes   No

* Our verse says that when we do that, we will suffer want. Has that ever been true in your life? How so or how not?

* Continue reading Jeremiah 17:7-8. Describe the state of the one who depends on God for his confidence.

* What is the effect on your soul when you put your hope in God instead of man?

* Name a time when you chose to put your hope in God over man. Where did that choice lead you?

* As a way to close your time of reflection today, take the space below to explore the ways you have looked to man to be a mirror for you, how that has affected you, and what you want to change in your perceptions.

Day Four: The Impact of Man

—Jewel for Your Journey—
*"Test everything that is said. Hold on to what
is good" (1 Thessalonians 5:21 NLT).*

Today is "field trip" day. Don't be disappointed, but you're not leaving your seat. Today we are taking a trip into the spheres of our hearts to check on the impact man has had on us. I promise you it's worth the trip—but you might want to wear your seat belt!

While yesterday's study emphasized the impermanence and fallibility of man, the truth is, man can have huge personal impact on us, both good and bad.

One of my favorite things to do is speak in public schools. Recently I spoke my "You Are More" message at a junior high school. As I was speaking I told the girls it's hard to believe "you are more" when men in your own home—especially your father—send you a "You Are Less" message. The moment I said this, a girl in the audience quickly got up and ran out crying. Later, when all the kids were gone, she and I huddled together on the gym floor and talked. She said her father had just left her family, and the last words he spoke to her were, "You are such a disappointment." This thirteen-year-old girl's chin began to quiver and her eyes rushed with stinging tears.

I looked her square in the eyes and told her she was not a disappointment; rather, he was. His words were reflections of his heart, not hers. I told her how beautiful and powerful she was, and how God loved her and had a plan for her life. I asked her what she loved to do, and she said she was a boxer. A fighter. I told her she had been knocked out—what was she going to do now? Bow out of the fight and believe she'd always stay down? No! She would get up and fight again, but first she had to decide her father was wrong about her. She had to believe God's voice above his. God says this girl has potential and promise, and no one can take that away from her. You should have seen her eyes light up with hope when she realized she had a future beyond the stinging blow of her father's words.

Man can wound us, but ultimately, it's up to us if we walk wounded. I, for one, walked wounded for too long. I allowed man's hurtful words and actions to embed themselves in my heart and grow nasty vines. Those vines shackled my heart, even years after I left the modeling industry. Often, my husband's words, which were not meant to hurt me, were filtered through the negative messages other men planted in my heart, and that became difficult for both of us. I had to identify the lies I had believed and embrace God's truth for me.

I don't know where you've been, my friend, but if your heart is beating, you've been hurt by man. It could be a mother who spoke scathing words to you or a father who abandoned, abused, or ignored you. It could be a former husband or boyfriend or boss or stranger who wounded you at one time or another. You may even be in a relationship with someone who is hurting you now.

* Have you ever been deeply hurt by man? Take the space below to describe that hurt. If there are many incidences of pain inflicted by others in your life, I want you to choose one that still hurts when you think about it.

* What would God say to you now about that hurt? Listen for his voice, and let him write to you here.

* How much do you allow man to be a measure of your value? Put an X on the line below:

I let man measure my value   I do not let man measure my value

_____

* How have you allowed man's words or actions to twist your sense of self-worth?

* What are some of the lies you've believed about yourself that have come from man?

* What impact does that lie have on your life now?

* What does God say to you about the lie(s)?

Identifying the lie you've believed, recognizing its impact, and replacing the lie with God's truth is essential to being free from it. The other key is forgiveness. Refusing to forgive man for his or her actions, words, and impact on us is a way to carry their sin forward. Their sin becomes a burdensome weight on our shoulders, wrecking our peace and joy. The load of other men's sin was never meant for us to carry. That's where Jesus comes in. He died for all sins for all men—including the one who hurt you.

* Use the space below to name areas of hurt that you want to forgive and commit them to the cross, where Jesus took on all men's sin. Trust that God can handle man. You don't need to carry his burden anymore.

* How do you think letting go of the offenses of the men in your life will affect your relationships?

I'd like to close out this day with another one of those straightforward Scriptures. Look back at today's Jewel for Your Journey. When we test the impact of man on our lives, we have to test it all. And while there has no doubt been some measure of pain, there is also a measure of goodness. This verse tells us not to hold on to the bad! It says we should hold on to the good! Many of us have people who have helped shape who we are in a wonderfully positive way. So I'd like to take a moment to focus on the good things man has brought into our lives and remember to hold onto truth rather than lies.

The best kind of people to surround ourselves with are those who reflect faith, hope, and love. They don't expect us to fill their cups and they don't try to fill ours either. God often speaks through these people messages of empowerment and even conviction. But ultimately, these people point us toward the Father for our strength.

* Think of a man or woman who has shaped your sense of value in a positive way. Recall some words or phrases that he or she spoke that instilled value in you.

* Name an action that a man or woman in your life has taken that has shown you how valuable you are.

* Now, record the impact of that person on your sense of value, identity, and purpose.

I encourage you to pray for the people who have seen the "more" and not the "less" in you. Thank God for them and thank them personally for their impact on your life as well.

It is my hope today that we turn away any fixed gaze we have on man and fix our eyes on God. In allowing him to be our strength and allowing him to declare our worth, we can love our fellow humans as Jesus did. Despite the rejection, accusations, and betrayal of man, he looked to the Father and found an unchanging reflection of his worth.

Lord, we pray that we too can look to you for our value. Thank you for the good people in our lives who have taught us what we look like in your eyes.

Day Five: The Prince and the Princess

—Jewel for Your Journey—

"It is better to take refuge in the LORD *than to trust
in people. It is better to take refuge in the* LORD
than to trust in princes" (Psalm 118:8-9).

I am so excited for you to meet with your girlfriend(s) today! Please keep in mind that this study can raise very sensitive subjects for other group members. Confidentiality is essential, and judgment is not allowed in church, remember? If someone in your group cries a living mess, think of Jesus and how he treated the sinful woman: He defended her, comforted her, and assured her of his presence and his promise.

Watch the video "The First Lie: You Are What Man Thinks of You" at www.jenniferstrickland.net. Use the space below for notes.

Week 2 The First Truth:

You Are a Beloved Daughter

Day One: Daughter

—Jewel for Your Journey—
"Yet you, LORD, are our Father" (Isaiah 64:8).

Read chapter 2 and use this space to journal your response. What did this chapter stir up in you? How did it make you feel? What or who did it make you think of and why?

Day Two: Loved

—Jewel for Your Journey—
"I put…a beautiful crown on your head" (Ezekiel 16:12).

As I say in the book, you cannot slouch with a crown on your head. That would make your crown fall right off, girl! The ironic thing about me saying this is I have a tendency to slouch. In fact, this was the reason my mother got me into modeling: I was trying to hide my height and she wanted me to stand up straight. Of course I had to stand tall while modeling, but years later, after three C-sections and being hunched over the kitchen sink, changing table, and keyboard for years, I found that I was slouching again. I realized there was also an emotional component to it: I was questioning my beauty and value, even doubting the calling of God on my life. On top of all that, I was carrying recent hurts, bending my back with the strain.

I opened my heart and let the hurts and doubts pour out to God as well as to a trusted handful of wise girlfriends. Over time my heart began to feel less weighty; I could lift it toward the sky instead of wrapping it in a shroud between my shoulders. I could also re-root my stance in the love of God and remember that I wore a crown, its jewels the signature of my authority and destiny. Next thing you knew, I was standing tall again, holding my head high.

From the crowns of our heads straight through our hearts and all the way to the tips of our toes, you and I are going to let God's unfailing love for his daughters seep into us over the course of the next three days. Let's pray.

Father, I pray that right now, we open our hearts to the feast you have laid out before us. I pray that today our hearts will be porous, like sponges soaking in your truth that heals and beautifies us. May our hearts become alive with the truth of your unfailing love.

* Please read Jeremiah 31:3-6. Write verse 3 here:

The Lord penned these words to imperfect, messy, sinful people. Their flawless behavior and sinless righteousness did not earn them his love and favor. Quite the contrary. They were messy and broken when he told them that they would be rebuilt. They were in mourning when he declared the day would come when they would dance with tambourines. Their land was desolate when he promised a future of fruitfulness. Despite their desperate state, he drew them to his abundance with gentle kindness. He loved them in spite of their sin; he believed in their greatness far before they were great. He saw their potential and told them what they could become long before it was true.

This is how he sees us. When I found the Lord, I was riddled with confusion. I barely knew which way was up. In that state, he declared his love to me. No matter what state you are in today, the Lord's love for you is unfailing, and he draws you to himself to help you become all that you are destined to be.

Let's take a close look at the story of the baby girl of Ezekiel. In the story, the Lord is addressing Jerusalem, which he likens to an abandoned and broken infant girl.

* Please read Ezekiel 16:1-5. In the first few verses, God refers to the little girl's parents, saying they were of pagan descent, coming from nations that were characterized by detestable practices and rampant evil. As a result, the baby girl was not cared for properly from the day she was born. Describe the condition of the baby girl:

* Read verses 6-7 and write here the word God speaks to her: _____ What do you think he is saying through this one word?

In verse 7, he makes her grow like "a plant of the field." If there were a name for the "seed" he planted in her that made her grow, what would you name it? Some might say it is faith. Some might say love. Some might say the Word he spoke to her fell into the soil of her heart and grew life. Whatever you think it is, I bet it's the same thing that makes you grow.

Keep reading her story in verse 8. One of the sweetest things God does for the little girl is cover her nakedness. Similarly, he made clothes for Adam and Eve to cover their nakedness when they left the garden (Genesis 3:21). This covering is a tender act of compassion, once again, not based on her behavior or righteousness, but based on the truth that ultimately, no matter where we've been, we are his children and he desires to remove all of our shame.

* What do you think is the meaning of his oath—or marriage-like covenant—to the girl who is now grown?

* He calls her "Mine." What does this mean to you?

* Read verses 9-14. What do you think these actions symbolize for her:

Bathing with water: _____

Washing off the blood: _____

Putting ointments on her: _____

* He goes on to clothe and dress her. Imagine here what her adornments symbolize:

Embroidered dress: _____

Leather sandals: _____

Fine linen and costly garments: _____

Jewelry: _____

Crown: _____

Because this story is so beautiful, I wanted you to read it in your own Bible first. But now I'd like you to read it in The Living Bible translation. The romance can't help but draw us:

> When you were born, no one cared for you. When I first saw you, your umbilical cord was uncut, and you had been neither washed nor rubbed with salt nor clothed. No one had the slightest interest in you; no one pitied you or cared for you. On that day when you were born, you were dumped out into a field and left to die, unwanted. But I came by and saw you there, covered with your own blood, and I said, "Live! Thrive like a plant in the field!" And you did! You grew up and became tall, slender and supple, a jewel among jewels. And when you reached the age of maidenhood, your breasts were full-formed and your pubic hair had grown; yet you were naked. Later, when I passed by and saw you again, you were old enough for marriage; and I wrapped my cloak around you to legally declare my marriage vow. I signed a covenant with you, and you became mine. Then, when the marriage had taken place, I gave you beautiful clothes of linens and silk, embroidered, and sandals made of dolphin hide. I gave you lovely ornaments, bracelets, and

beautiful necklaces, a ring for your nose and two more
for your ears, and a lovely tiara for your head. And so
you were made beautiful with gold and silver, and your
clothes were silk and linen and beautifully embroidered.
You ate the finest foods and became more beautiful than
ever. You looked like a queen, and so you were! Your rep-
utation was great among the nations for your beauty; it
was perfect because of all the gifts I gave you.

* Is there anything in your experience that relates to the baby girl
  who grows into a powerful queen? Explain.

   This bloody, bruised, and broken girl was rescued by a God who
saw her. He saw beyond her present state and believed in who she
could be. His love washes us of our past and dresses us in promise.
   Turn to Isaiah and read chapter 61.

* Focusing on verses 3 and 10, what do you think is the meaning
  of the new garments he gives us?

   Now, read Isaiah 62:1-5.
   Here, the Lord speaks about Jerusalem again. He says he will
not remain quiet until she is all she was created to be. He will not
rest until her glory shines like the dawn. Do you see how he adores
and believes in his people, even when we are in our most desperate, destructive places? Regardless of our stained and torn, worn-
out clothes, he says to us, "I'll marry you. Be mine, and I will dress
you in praise."

* What are the "old names" he gives Jerusalem in verse 4? What are her new names?

* What does he mean when he says we are his bride? What does a bride look like?

* Use the space below to list key words to describe what we were and what we can be. I have started the list for you!

Baby Girl	Radiant Bride
Thrown Out	Rescued
Rejected	Delighted in
Bloody	Washed

Faith changes us. Hope transforms us. Love redeems us. I am thankful for a God who sees us in our solitude and sweeps us off our feet with love. I am thankful for a God who crowns us in his compassion. It is my hope for both of us today that we wear that crown well. Today, let us stand straight and raise our hearts to the sky.

Day Three: Our Rock of Refuge

—Jewel for Your Journey—

*"Truly he is my rock and my salvation; he is my
fortress, I will never be shaken" (Psalm 62:2).*

I'm so looking forward to our study today because it is going to be
very restful, and I love to rest! My favorite time of the day (aside
from writing) is climbing into bed and pulling the sheets over me.
Mmm, delicious. In the busyness of life, I *crave* quiet. I love it when
the kids are in bed and I get to kick my feet up with a cup of coffee
or tea and a blanket and just sit still. Better yet, I love having a Bible
in my lap. No distractions, no hurry, just a candle, a journal, and a
Bible. That time fills my soul like nothing else.

It is during this time that I seek the Lord and he meets me wherever I am. I hope you too experience magical moments when you
seek him and find him. If only we would run to him first, always; if
only his voice rose above all other voices, always; if only he were our
refuge and hiding place from the storm and rain, always.

Our study of "man" has told us his life is but a breath while God's
Word stands eternal. We have looked at verses that have warned us
not to make man our refuge. Instead, look to an Almighty God.
But let's be real: It's easier to look to what we *can* see than what we
can't see. When storms come, I'm as susceptible as anyone else to
run to people for comfort and security before I run to God. The
best people to run to, of course, are those whose security comes
from him—because they point us back to his Word and back to his
supremacy.

Today we're going to call God our Rock of refuge as we read
some of David's songs to him—songs written by a soul who battled
with men but found victory in God.

* Read Psalm 62. What do you think David is struggling with in verses 3 and 4?

* In his humility, David considered his kingship to be a "leaning wall," a "tottering fence." His throne was uncertain, in his mind, but God was his certainty. What does it mean in your life for God to be your fortress?

* Do you let man "shake you" (verse 6)? Why?

* In The Living Bible translation, verses 7-9 read, "My protection and success come from God alone. He is my refuge, a Rock where no enemy can reach me. O my people, trust him all the time. Pour out your longings before him, for he can help! The greatest of men or the lowest—both alike are nothing in his sight. They weigh less than air on scales." What contrast is David drawing between man and God here?

Read Psalm 18:1-19, the words David sang when the Lord delivered him from the hand of all his enemies and from the hand of Saul.

✳ List the names David gives God in the first two verses:

✳ What response do you have to the rest of this passage?

This is a special passage of Scripture for me. I read it the year after I found Christ, and my jaw dropped. It described my experience with God in the Black Forest of Germany, where I had gone for a week to give my life to him. "He reached down from on high and took hold of me; he drew me out of deep waters. He rescued me from my powerful enemy, from my foes, who were too strong for me…He brought me out into a spacious place; he rescued me because he delighted in me" (verses 16-17,19).

I remember feeling like I needed something bigger than myself to rescue me. All my life I had depended on myself and my strength, but the forces opposing me were too strong. I knew I needed God, and I was a broken fence before him. Isn't it beautiful that when we are crumbling, he parts the heavens and soars on the wings of the wind to save us because he *delights* in us?

I wonder if part of our problem is not just trusting "man" or "princes" to save us; but putting confidence in ourselves. It's believing we can make our dreams come true. We can heal, save, and rescue ourselves—we have all the answers. We can become so out-of-touch with our own frailty that we can become our own "rocks."

The times I've tried to do life on my own, I've ended up broken. But when I let him have the troubles of my life and do things his way, I am strengthened and victorious.

* Continue reading Psalm 18:30-36. What does God do for those who take refuge in him?

* The Word teaches us that man is dust, so standing on man for our solace is like standing on sand. But God is our Rock, our solid foundation. What does it mean to *you* to make God your Rock?

* How about making God your shield?

* Let's close our study today by reading Psalm 144 in its entirety. Write here the kinds of blessings in store for those who make God their Rock, their fortress, their stronghold, their deliverer, their shield, and their refuge:

Sometimes just soaking in the life-giving words of the Psalms is the best nourishment you can give yourself. What a gift today has been.

I pray today we both can stand, hearts raised, on the Rock, saying the words of our brother David: "He alone is my fortress. I will never be shaken!"

Day Four: Secure in Love

—Jewel for Your Journey—

*"Let the beloved of the LORD rest secure in him, for he
shields him all day long, and the one the LORD loves
rests between his shoulders" (Deuteronomy 33:12).*

I am such a natural-born people-pleaser that getting my security from God alone is about as natural as standing on my head. I can do it; it's possible. But it's not something I can sustain for very long without concentrated effort.

Making God our refuge is not our first instinct. Our first instinct is to get our security from man. It's easier to put our faith in what we can see than what we can't see. Those of us who have looked to men for security and been either betrayed or disappointed have to try doubly hard. The failures of our fathers, husbands, mothers, brothers, or friends, however, do not point to the inadequacy of God. We must remember that man is made in God's image; God is not made in man's image. All men fall short of the glory of God, but as for God, his way is perfect (Romans 3:23; Psalm 18:30). He is a secure fortress. His love is perfectly unfailing, and he is our Father with a capital "F."

* Read Isaiah 9:6 and write the names of Christ below:

* We are his daughters, and we find out who we are in the reflection of who he is. If his name is "Everlasting Father," what does that say of us? Circle one:

We are his beloved daughters...

> **for our lifetimes on earth**
>
> **for as long as we do things right**
>
> **for eternity**

You got that one right, sister. Of course, I did make it pretty simple for you! But knowing that he is our eternal father and we are his eternal daughters may shift the places we look to for security. Man's life is brief, so he is not to be our source of security. Man can instill value in us and he can be *a* source of security, but he is not *the* source.

In Isaiah 63:16, the prophet writes, "You, LORD, are our Father, our Redeemer from of old is your name." A redeemer is one who buys back, one who repurchases, one who frees us from distress, harm, or captivity. As our Redeemer who bought us back with his blood, God will free us from any distress or harm caused by man. Furthermore, he will use it for his glory if we so ask and believe. Our God will redeem every curse from man. He will wipe every tear from our eye and restore our hearts to wholeness.

One of our goals in this study is to practice turning away from what we can see and turn instead toward what we can't see for our beauty, value, strength, and identity. But one thing we can see is that which God has made—his Creation and his Word. Both tell us a lot about the kind of Father he is.

 * Read Psalm 145:8 and write here some of the characteristics of God:

 * Since we know from 1 John 4:8 that "God is love," let's look at God's definition of love in 1 Corinthians 13:4-7. Write the characteristics of his love here:

* Song of Songs 2:4 says, "Let his banner over me be love." Use this space to draw a picture of what that looks like to you:

I hope you know today how much he loves you. If the picture still isn't clear, let's remember another verse from 1 John: "This is how God showed his love among us: He sent his one and only Son into the world that we might live through him. This is love: not that we loved God, but that he loved us and sent his Son as an atoning sacrifice for our sins" (1 John 4:9-10).

* What is the nature of God's love for his children?

We have a Father who gave up his only child so that we could be his children. We have a Father who is willing to wipe our slates clean of everything that has damaged our relationship with him. We have a Father whose love is so unfailing that nothing can separate us from it.

Please read Ephesians 3:14-19, Paul's prayer for the Ephesians. This is my prayer for both of us, my sister, my friend—that we could be strengthened with power through his Spirit in our inner beings, so that Christ may dwell in our hearts through faith. And that we would grasp how wide, long, high, and deep is the love of God, and become firmly established in it.

* What does it mean to be rooted and established in love? How might that even affect our posture?

* What would it look like to you to walk as a woman who is deeply loved by God?

* How might that affect your relationships? If it helps here to focus on one significant relationship, then do that.

The more established a tree is, the stronger, healthier, and more fruitful it is. As women who pursue God, we must be intentional about rooting ourselves not in man, but in the love of God. Like the tree planted by streams of living water of Psalm 1:1-3, I pray we root ourselves in his love.

He loved us when we were a mess. He believes in us now, despite whatever is still messy in our lives. He raises our heads, raises our hearts, and says, "I am your root. I will make you grow. I will wash you off. I will beautify you. For you are my Daughter, and no matter where you are in the race, you wear a victor's crown."

* Please close this day of study by reading Deuteronomy 33:12. This is a tender verse that I want you to really take in. You, my sister, are "the beloved of the LORD." Imagine yourself climbing up like a little girl into the Father's lap and resting your head between his strong shoulders. What would it look like for you to rest secure in the Father's love?

Father, help us to remember that in your unfailing love, you call us "Mine." Help us to root ourselves in your unfailing love. Help us to walk as women who know who they are—the beloved daughters of the King. We are the beloved of the Lord. Help us to put our security and confidence only in you.

Day Five: The King's Daughter

—Jewel for Your Journey—
"Daughter, your faith has made you well. Go in peace, and be healed of your affliction" (Mark 5:34 NKJV).

I am so looking forward to sharing this message with you face-to-face via the video. This message is transforming. Don't miss it!

Watch the video "The First Truth: You Are a Beloved Daughter" at www.jenniferstrickland.net. Use the space below for notes.

Week 3 The Second Lie:

You Are What You See in the Mirror

Day One: Mirror, Mirror

— Jewel for Your Journey —
"Our struggle is not against flesh and blood" (Ephesians 6:12).

Read chapter 3. What did this chapter make you think about? How did it make you feel?

* What in this chapter is similar or dissimilar to your own experience? Explain.

The mirror can be so captivating for us that we begin to believe it is a reflection of our value, beauty, purpose, and position. But in the coming days we are going to see that while the reflection in the mirror is a part of who we are, it is nowhere near the sum of our worth.

If you or someone you know suffers from an eating disorder— overeating included—I want you to believe with me that healing is possible. But we must remember "our struggle is not against flesh and blood, but against the rulers, against the authorities, against the powers of this dark world and against the spiritual forces of evil in the heavenly realms" (Ephesians 6:12). Biblically, the body is a symbol for the church, so when women "hate" or reject their bodies, they are succumbing to a lie promoted by the enemy, who hates the church, despises God's creation, and wants to convince us it's not good enough.

Your battle and our daughters' battles with their bodies are really not conflicts with the flesh. They are wars of the spirit. And when we have a combat of the spirit, our best weapon is prayer. So let's pray.

Gracious and compassionate Father, you know our battle. You know our pain, in the body and in the heart, in the mind and in the soul. You know the wrong places we look for our worth, and we know you are the right place. In your eyes, we are so much more than what we see in the mirror. Help us to balance outward beauty with the inward woman. As a weight on a scale, help us measure ourselves and others not in pounds or inches but by the weight of who you are.

In the power of Jesus Christ, I sever any bondage I and the women reading this have to an unhealthy relationship with the mirror, the scale, the measuring tape, and food. In Jesus's name and by the working of his blood, I ask that you bond us to our Creator for our true reflection and teach us to live in these bodies healthfully so your life will be seen through us.

Help us to see as you see, and help us live as you desire us to live. In Jesus's name, amen.

Day Two: Our Bodies

—Jewel for Your Journey—

"Though outwardly we are wasting away, yet inwardly we are being renewed day by day" (2 Corinthians 4:16).

Remember, this is not a Bible study about anyone else but you and God! It's a journey to a stronger, healthier, more powerful you in light of a mighty Father and Creator. But here's the truth: no pain, no gain!

Lately I've been doing workouts on DVD. This is what I've discovered about workouts: There's a lot of pain involved! But there's also a lot of gain. By submitting my body to the exercise, my vitality and strength are increased for everything else I do.

The same goes with our time with the Lord. By making time to submit our hearts to him, we discover great gain. But in order to experience the gain, we have to be willing to be honest about the pain. In the words of Paul, "We have spoken freely to you, Corinthians, and opened wide our hearts to you...Open wide your hearts also" (2 Corinthians 6:11,13).

Opening our hearts can leave us feeling vulnerable, but we won't be left there to stay. Being honest with God is kind of like seeing a doctor who will only tell you the truth. He's not going to pretend an illness doesn't exist, so we can't either. When we come to him, we have to allow him to take a transparent look at our hearts and make an accurate, truthful diagnosis. If infection exists, we must allow him the course of treatment to heal it. He may want to open the area around the infection and reconnect pieces so life can flow. He may administer life-giving medicine. He may want to wash and cleanse the wound for a long time before he closes it up. Then, he will treat the wound with care—not pretending it was never there, but instead nurturing it and checking on it periodically. Over time, the area will heal. The honesty, the diagnosis, the treatment, and the follow-up made us better!

Are you treatable? Are you ready and willing to open your heart so that God can touch the thing in you that only he can see? The thing he wants to heal?

I think I just heard a "yes" but you may have barely whispered it. So let's open today's study in prayer.

Compassionate Healer, thank you for being with us on this journey today. Open our hearts for your touch. Speak to us so that not only do we hear with our ears, but your words are impressed upon our souls. Despite the many noises and people who clamor for our attention, we press in now like the bleeding woman, believing you and only you can heal us. In your face we see our true reflection: Daughter. Loved. Healed. Whole. Help us to live your truth. Amen.

✱ Let's begin with a foundational truth which will get us through the next two weeks of study. Please read Isaiah 64:8 and write it here:

Now, please glance up and read your "jewel" for today's journey.

Honestly I'm not sure if that "jewel" was encouraging or depressing, but it's a precious stone on our pathway nonetheless. These words were scribed by Paul in his second letter to the Corinthian church. Paul had recently suffered a painful visit with them in which he was insulted and rejected by false teachers who had cropped up in the church. Although the majority of the people had since repented from their rebellion, Paul was wise to know division still existed and their painful history had not been totally healed.

The theme of this letter is how to navigate suffering with the power of the Spirit in our lives. Yet not only does it address the battles this ambassador of Christ endured, but it also gives us profound insight into the battle with our bodies.

✱ Read 2 Corinthians 4:7-10. Notice that we are told here we have a treasure in "jars of clay"—that is, our bodies. What is the treasure that gives us "all-surpassing power"? Circle one.

Regular workouts   Makeovers   The Holy Spirit   Medicine

The answer is obvious, although many miss this essential truth. Lots of people focus their energy on the flesh while ignoring the treasure within.

Looking at verses 8 and 9, list the words that describe our battle on the left and the end result for us on the right. I have started the list for you. If you feel so led, look up other translations to add other words to our list.

We are...
Hard pressed on every side   **Not crushed**

* What does verse 10 say we carry within our mortal bodies?

We carry around the death of Jesus so the life of Jesus can be made manifest in us. This is why even a deadly disease doesn't conquer us—because in the scope of eternity, we are unconquerable. The life of Jesus lives in us eternally, and whether we are healed on earth or in heaven, we will live on, forever, in his presence.

* Please read 2 Corinthians 4:16-18. Why do you think Paul, the writer, tells us here not to "lose heart"?

* Why should we not fix our eyes on what is "seen"?

In this passage, Paul is encouraging the Corinthians to not focus on the distress, grief, and heartache of the present moment. He is saying, Don't give up! Don't get discouraged! Jesus is going to come back for us and take us to glory. On the outside, we may waste away, but the life inside our mortal bodies renews us day by day. That life inside of us is the life of a risen Christ.

Please turn your Bible to the book of Isaiah and read chapter 52:13-15 and chapter 53, the beautiful prophecies Isaiah wrote about the Christ. We are going to delve deeper in this passage in the coming weeks, but today I want you to focus on just a few choice morsels.

* What do we learn in verse 53:2 about Jesus's outward appearance?

* According to 52:14, what happened to Jesus's physical appearance on the cross?

* List the words used to describe him in verses 3-5.

* What is the one word used to describe *us* in this passage? Circle one:

Crushed   Bruised   Despised   Rejected   Healed

* Read verse 5 and fill in the blank: By his _____ we are _____.

* Is there an area in your body that is wounded, afflicted or suffering and needs to be healed? If so, please write it here:

* Is there an area in your heart that is wounded, afflicted or suffering and needs to be healed? If so, please write it here:

* I want you to close this day of study asking the Healer for his diagnosis and treatment for whatever is afflicting you. Write what he tells your spirit here.

Diagnosis:

Treatment:

The good news is that with Christ you can be healed. Receive the immensity of his love for you today. As his daughter, you carry his death in your mortal body so that his eternal life may be revealed through you. Don't get so caught up in the body (which is temporary) that you miss the eternal treasure within you. His life planted in you is your most sacred treasure. Nurture the treasure, because while outwardly we are wasting away, he renews us day by day.

Day Three: The Mirror and Me

— Jewel for Your Journey —

"We live by faith, not by sight" (2 Corinthians 5:7).

Well begin this day of study with a passage of Scripture you are becoming quite familiar with. You've heard me speak about it, you've read my characterization of it in the book...but now I want you to read the life-giving words in your Bible. Something new about you or about Christ may just stand out to you. Please read Mark 5:21-43.

* In verse 23, what does the father Jairus believe will heal his daughter?

* In Isaiah 52, the prophet says that Jesus will be a suffering servant. How does that make his relationship to the bleeding woman more intimate?

* What happened when the bleeding woman reached out?

The same power that healed the bleeding woman is at work in us now—that "all-surpassing power" that gives us strength and renewal no matter what we are facing.

* What do Jesus's words in verse 36 say to you today?

* What touches you most about the story of the little girl?

I could gush all over the place about how tender our Lord is. He raises a little girl to life; he looks for the suffering woman in the crowd and blesses her with peace; he picks us up out of the rubble and says, "You are more because I love you."

These people had to believe what they couldn't see. They had to trust what had not yet been proven.

We are now going to turn back to Paul's second letter to the Corinthians. He's not yet done talking to us about Christ's risen power in these bodies of ours. Read 2 Corinthians 5:1-10, keeping in mind that the "earthly tent" is our body and the "eternal house" is our heavenly, risen, perfect body.

To help us out even more, I've included verses 1-7 in The Message version below:

> We know that when these bodies of ours are taken down like tents and folded away, they will be replaced by resurrection bodies in heaven—God-made, not hand-made—and we'll never have to relocate our "tents" again. Sometimes we can hardly wait to move—and so we cry out in frustration. Compared to what's coming, living conditions around here seem like a stopover in an unfurnished shack, and we're tired of it! We've been given a glimpse of the real thing, our true home, our resurrection bodies! The Spirit of God whets our appetite

by giving us a taste of what's ahead. He puts a little of heaven in our hearts so that we'll never settle for less. That's why we live with such good cheer. You won't see us drooping our heads or dragging our feet! Cramped conditions here don't get us down. They only remind us of the spacious living conditions ahead. It's what we trust in but don't yet see that keeps us going.

Although The Message version has helped me understand this passage better, I still love the words "groan" and "longing to be clothed with our heavenly dwelling" from the NIV. These words helped me heal from my anger at the imperfections in the mirror. They made me realize that I longed for perfection and I needed to surrender to the fact it couldn't be found on earth. We "groan and are burdened" because we seek the perfection of heaven.

* When it comes to your body, what burdens you? Is it the mirror or a sickness or a size or shape? Describe it here.

* Please write verse 7 here:

This is a tough one when it comes to our bodies because we see them all the time. We experience firsthand what's right and what's not right. We can either choose to focus on what we can see or turn our attention to what we can't see, which is where the real power to either change or accept our bodies comes from.

* When it comes to your burden or battle with your body, what unhealthy ways do you focus on what you can see?

The more we fixate on something, the larger it gets. "As [a man] thinks in his heart, so is he," Proverbs 23:7 tells us (NKJV). So if a woman tells herself all the time, "I am fat, I am fat, I am fat," guess what? She becomes fat. If a woman says, "I am old, I am old, I am old," she begins to behave, feel, and look old. The power of the mind and our thoughts profoundly influence the body.

* What "I am" statements do you make about yourself that are manifesting themselves in your body, good or bad?

I know a girl who lost 200 pounds. Before she lost the weight, she decided she was beautiful. In response to her accepting that truth, she began looking beautiful in every way. That one truth—as well as some hard work—transformed her body. She lost the weight long after she decided who and what she was.

* What "I am" statements could you begin making to shift the way you perceive yourself and possibly shift your body's response to your thoughts?

* What are you doing to win your personal battle regarding your body in a healthy way? Circle all that apply.

Lifting weights

Taking yoga, pilates, or aerobics classes

Enjoying the outdoors

Drinking lots of water

Taking vitamins

Seeing your doctor regularly

Caring well for your skin

Eating and drinking healthfully

Sometimes we get so busy caring for everyone else that we don't take the time to care for ourselves as much as we should. Personally, I find that if I do the above things, I am stronger, happier, and healthier for my family. I'm sure you agree.

Yet there are other components of our health that we must not miss—the health of our spirit and soul. The spirit is the part of us that becomes alive when we accept Christ. The soul is composed of three parts: the mind (the thinker), the will (the chooser), and the emotions (the feeler). Caring for our bodies, spirits, and souls are equally important.

* Now, I want you to do some practical application. Name three ways you can better take care of yourself *this week* for each part of you:

Your body:

Your spirit:

Your soul:

     Mind:

     Will:

     Emotions:

I've got my assignment for the week written down; I hope you do too. This week, I plan to go to yoga, take a walk, and make a long overdue OB appointment. For my spirit, I plan to be in the Word, praying daily, and rooting myself in the river of God's love. For my soul? Mind: Take my thoughts captive to make them obedient to Christ. Will: Submit my will to the Father's. Emotions: Ask the Holy Spirit to govern my emotions by helping me choose love in my interactions with people.

Whatever your list looks like, it's right on. It's exactly what you need for this week.

Father, thank you for making us body, soul, and spirit. Thank you for making our dead spirits alive. Help us to feed these bodies, souls, and spirits with exactly what they need to grow and blossom and become more beautiful with time. Renew us in every way. In your Son's precious name, amen.

Day Four: Like Mother, Like Daughter

—Jewel for Your Journey—
*"These older women must train the
younger women" (Titus 2:4 NLT).*

One time my pastor's wife gave me a beautiful poem about how children are a reflection of their mothers. I had it tacked to my corkboard behind my computer for about a year. But then one day I was at the grocery store with my four-year-old son. Donning his Yoda costume and a light saber, he was running through the aisles like a wild man, ignoring my every demand to return to my side and act appropriately.

After this experience, I decided the poem was untrue and took it down. My child is not a reflection of me; my child is a reflection of God, and I am given authority to guide him in the directions of God's plan for his life...one of them being self-control. Don't worry—I didn't let him get away with it in the grocery store, but I had to laugh at the thought that his behavior was a reflection of me.

I have contemplated that poem many times over the years, especially when in the company of one special mother I know. Her daughter has chosen to embrace tattoos, marijuana, joblessness, and lesbianism. Her daughter has spent most of her life in unrest, aimlessness, and loneliness, whereas the mother has modeled all her life the nature of God by way of her faith, gentleness, wisdom, and radiant, praying spirit. This mother prays unceasingly for her daughter, whose life is slowly being transformed into a life of faith.

Are children really made in the image of their mothers? No: None of us are made in the image of man. We are all *imago dei*—made in the image of God—and our choices are our choices, not our mothers'. Nevertheless, mothers wield a great deal of influence over our daughters, and just as we have the potential to pass on a life of faith, we can pass on generational bondages that cripple our girls in even greater ways than they crippled us.

My bondages were with men and mirrors. I looked to men for affirmation, and if I wasn't looking to them, I was looking at the mirror. A perfectionist myself, I went on to marry a perfectionist! Our first child, Olivia, was on a perfect schedule, had a perfect room, and had a perfect outfit all the time! What a recipe for—you guessed it—*perfectionism*.

One day, she began noticing every stray hair in her ponytail and every wrinkle in her bedcover. Even the slight itch of a tag on a T-shirt was grounds for emotional upheaval. We dealt with these issues as they came about. But it seemed the day she started junior high, she lingered far too long in front of the mirror. I tried everything—telling her to turn away, physically turning her away, having Dad tell her to stop looking at herself...None of it worked.

Then one day I asked God what to do about it. He led me to join her in the bathroom. What I found was this: She was comforted by my mere presence in the bathroom. She battles less with the mirror when I am simply in the room, supporting her. So, as much as possible, morning coffee in hand, I just "hang out" in the bathroom with her. I see that if I affirm her and love her and touch her, she is less demanding of that stubborn reflection in the mirror—and quicker to walk away from it.

* What responsibility do you think mothers have when it comes to their daughter's self-image?

* If you have a daughter or other young person in your life who you wield influence over, how do you suppose you can help that person understand their value?

* Please read Titus 2:3-4. What is our responsibility to the next generation? What specifically do we need to teach younger women?

* Please read 1 Samuel 16:7. How do you think the younger generation of girls struggles to live this truth?

Today, I am giving you a greater assignment. I would like for you to take some time today to speak into the heart and life of a younger woman or girl. We older women have a responsibility to teach what is good to the young women. I want you to tell a young woman the truth of how God sees her. I bet it won't take long for someone special to come to mind. Write her a note or give her a call. In a world that obsesses over outward appearance, it will be refreshing for her to know you see her heart.

Creator God, you created each person in your image. Whether or not we feel like we measure up to our earthly standards, we are yours, reflections of your heart. Help us today to love one of your daughters, to share with her what we know is true: She is made in your image, loved and precious in your sight. May our words to her be breath and life to her soul. Amen.

Day Five: Healed

—Jewel for Your Journey—

"Now we see only a reflection as in a mirror; then we shall see face to face" (1 Corinthians 13:12).

Meet with your group and watch the video "The Second Lie: You Are What You See in the Mirror" at www.jenniferstrickland.net. Use the space below for notes.

Week 4 The Second Truth:

You Are a Precious Creation

Day One: Precious

— Jewel for Your Journey —

"You are not your own; you were bought at a price. Therefore honor God with your bodies" (1 Corinthians 6:19-20).

Read chapter 4. What stood out to you most from this chapter?

* What in this chapter do you relate to in your experience?

* How can you share the message of this chapter with the younger generation?

This is going to be a great week of study. We will dig deep into the Word, and on the final day you will take your own "adventure in creation." So plan ahead. Think about what you enjoy doing in the outdoors and plan to make time for it. My prayers are with you!

Day Two: The Creator

—Jewel for Your Journey—

"In him all things were created: things in heaven and on earth, visible and invisible, whether thrones or powers or rulers or authorities; all things have been created through him and for him" (Colossians 1:16).

It's natural for us to look at the speckled canopy of the stars and say, "Wow, God's creation is amazing!" It's easy to look at the sweet face of a chubby baby and say, "Isn't he perfect?" But for most of us it's hard to look at ourselves in the mirror, and say, "Wow! Magnificent!"

In fact, I'm writing this passage from an airplane, and I just got up to use the restroom. In these situations I try to take a quick glance in the mirror but I accidentally lingered there for thirty seconds too long. In the up-close reflection, I saw age spots I honestly don't believe were there yesterday. "Yikes!" I gasped.

In a world fixated on images of "flawless" skin and ageless perfection and a cupboard full of potions claiming such, I make the conscious choice to turn away from the mirror. I won't lie and tell you I'm satisfied with my reflection. I'm not. I still wish it had no flaw. So for now, I'm determined to be the best I can be in the skin that I'm in.

We all have our own kind of longing in the body—the desire to be completely unburdened and free. And someday we will be. But perfection in heaven is real because we experience not just the absence of disease and aching bones, but because we will be filled to the brim with the fullness of God. The Father, the Son, and the Spirit will be all we need, flowing in endless abundance. As 1 Corinthians

13:10 puts it, "When the time of perfection comes, these partial things will become useless" (NLT). This is true of the body, soul, and spirit. Whatever is lacking in us now will be transformed to glory.

* Read 1 Corinthians 13:12. The context of this verse is Paul's famous teaching on the power of love to surpass all things. He says here that this life is like a dim, cloudy reflection in a mirror. When we look in the mirror it seems like a perfect reflection, but Paul says it's not. In what way can a mirror actually be a poor reflection?

There are two essential things we must know about the mirror. It's always changing and it's never satisfied. Something that is always changing cannot possibly be an accurate reflection of who we are. If we rely on something that is ever-changing to define us, we will always walk on insecure footing. Let's be reminded of Malachi 3:6: "I the LORD do not change." Basing our identity on a reflection that does not change will provide us with a secure foundation. Rather than building on shifting sand, we can build on the Rock—which will stand the test of time.

Today we are going to turn away from the mirror and take a close look at our Creator, remembering that in the reflection of his face we get a clearer picture of who we are and how to live. Deuteronomy 32:6 asks, "Is he not your Father, your Creator, who made you and formed you?"

* Read Psalm 146:6 and write here what God is called:

* The first thing the Word says about God is that he is the Creator. From a formless and empty earth, he created everything. Please read Genesis 1:1–2:2, allowing these living words to penetrate you. After reading this, what is your impression of God as Creator?

* What does he see when he looks at his creation?

It's important to notice how many times the Word says God looked at his creation and saw that it was "good." After he separated water from sky, and dry ground from seas, he "saw that it was good." After he created the sun, moon, and stars, he "saw that it was good." After he created the creatures of the sea and sky, he "saw that it was good." And after he made the wild animals, "God saw that it was good."

* Jump forward to Genesis 2:18. What is the only thing God says is "not good"?

To remedy the situation, God created woman to be man's helpful companion. Because there are two congruous accounts of the creation, we are now going to look back to the first account to see what he said after he completed man and woman.

* Write the first sentence of Genesis 1:31 here:

Aha! Now, creation isn't just good—it's *very* good!

* According to Genesis 1:27, what is different about the creation of man, both male and female?

We are the only created beings made after the likeness of God. In light of this, isn't it a shame that we can be so dissatisfied with our appearance? God created woman as the final act of creation. We are literally the tipping point from his view of "good" to "very good."

In my opinion, the influx of airbrushed and computerized female images, as well as the increase of self-promotion and self-worship, have greatly contributed to the skyrocketing number of women and girls who are dissatisfied with their appearance. Not a day goes by when a woman or girl isn't faced with an altered image personifying female beauty. Statistics show we see over 500 media images a day. Yet not enough of these images reveal multi-ethnic, plus-size, aged, short, or average-looking women and girls.

The world God first created has become plastered with images of women that none of us resemble in real life. What does this have to do with God as Creator? A lot!

* Read Romans 1:20. How do we see God's divinity and power?

If we do not honor God as Creator, we are without excuse. God's power is made known by what he made—by what we *see*. We don't only have to study him through the Word; we also have his creation. The creation isn't something we have to believe "by faith." This is something we can see, touch, feel, and experience.

Yet something sinister happens to our hearts when we do not honor God as our Creator.

* Read Romans 1:21-25. What happened to the hearts of those who would not glorify God or give thanks to him?

* In verse 24, what is the result of this worship of human images?

As much as it's easier not to look at this verse, the truth is, we live in a culture that worships image and, in turn, is overcome with sexual impurity.

* According to verse 25, how do we exchange the truth about God for a lie?

In our culture, people worship and serve created things instead of the Creator. We exchange the temporary for the eternal. We worship man or the mirror instead of God. And what is the impact? Our foolish hearts become darkened.

* Ecclesiastes 12:1 advises you to "Remember your Creator in the days of your youth." How can you stop today and remember your Creator? What would you like to say to him now?

Precious Creator, sometimes in our angst we forget you. We willingly trade in the beautiful truth for a lie. We bow down to false images. Yet they do not make our hearts happy or fulfilled. You do! You are our source, our Creator, who made what is good and who is pleased with it. Help us to see ourselves in the reflection of your power, your glory, and your might. In Jesus's name, amen.

Day Three: The Creation

— Jewel for Your Journey —

"I praise you because I am fearfully and wonderfully made; your works are wonderful, I know that full well" (Psalm 139:14).

I have the privilege today to be writing from our family ranch. My husband's parents just bought the land, establishing a future legacy for our children. The terrain is uncut, raw, and vast. There is no house yet on the property, so we have rented a trailer for a long weekend and are camping.

I woke up this morning creaky and slightly cranky from a poor night of sleep in the trailer, and the moment I opened my eyes I glimpsed an endless golden meadow and a hot orange rising sun. The morning mist still hovered over the field, and I listened to the stillness of the landscape, breathing a great big sigh of relief. Hawks, quail, doves, cattle, coyotes, and armadillos are the creatures we enjoy here. The meadows flutter with golden butterflies and the thicket of woods offers faint sightings of white-tailed deer. At night, the stars shine brighter than any I've seen. The ranch will be our getaway, our beautiful and brilliant canvas, our refuge from the busy world, and our reminder that God created the beauty of the mountains, hills, valleys, forests and fields for us to explore. He poured out the waterfalls, filled the lakes, created the rivers, and made the massive oceans teeming with life. He is our Creator and we are given both dominion over and participation in his grand creation.

* Please read Psalm 104 in its entirety. What act of creation do verses 5-9 refer to?

* What do verses 10-16 tell us about our Creator?

God doesn't just create life; he also sustains life. He gives water to the beasts of the field; a place for the birds of the air to nest; grass for the cattle to feed; and plants for man to cultivate.

From the comfort of my home, his creation is sweetly enjoyed as I walk on the trails near my neighborhood and weave along trickling streams, not far from city streets. If I need food, I go to the store. But out on the raw land, life is hard. Just this weekend on the ranch, the children found cattle bones, the springs ran low from drought, and when our generator ran out, cooking a simple dinner came down to gathering wood—a lot of work compared to what is normally easy at home. When we ran out of water, we washed with cold, wet rags. We hacked away at thorny vines of thorns to bring out the beauty of the trees, and Shane got cut all over his arms. I kept thinking about

Adam and Eve and the pilgrims and the Indians, and how hard they worked to tame the earth and bring forth its fruits.

If you've seen villages made of mud huts, encountered lions on the Sahara, or experienced a wild storm at sea, you know God's creation is not just glorious; it's fierce.

* According to today's psalm…

   Where do the lions get their food? (verse 21) _____
   What was man created to do? (verse 23) _____
   Who sustains us? (verses 27-30) _____
   Write verse 31 here. We will refer to it later.

Now, read Isaiah 40:21-31. I love the challenge God gives us here: "To whom will you compare me? Or who is my equal?" To answer the question, he tells us to look to the creation. He says, Do you see this? Do you know who created all of this?

* What does he say in verses 27-31 to those who question him, complaining that God cannot see them?

* What do verses 29-31 say to you?

Flip back and read Psalm 139:1-16. In this psalm, David answers the complaint in Isaiah 40:27. The Word says to us here, God knows our thoughts; he knows when we lie down and when we get up; he is familiar with all our ways.

* What do the first ten verses of Psalm 139 mean to you personally?

* What do verses 13-16 say to you on an intimate level?

I hope these words are water to your soul, as they are to mine. Did he make us? Yes. Does he know us? Yes. Do we discover who we are in the bathroom mirror? No. We see who we are and what we are worth in the mirror of God—his creation and his Word.

My friend, wherever you are in your journey, know that he made you and he knows what you need. He sustains you, and when he ushers you to come home to him, you will see his face and know fully.

Glance back up now and read Psalm 104:31, which you wrote down. This is one of my favorite verses, and we could have easily missed it. But we must pay attention to it, because we are "made in his image." We are created in the likeness of God. We are *like* him, and when we work hard on something, giving our heart to it—whether it's writing a book or knitting a blanket or creating a landscape or building a home or performing a dance—the most satisfying reward is to be able to rejoice in it. Tasting the fruit of our labor, seeing how it blesses or moves others, makes the whole work worthwhile.

You, my friend, are his work, his masterpiece, and he rejoices in the creation of you. He does not look at you and see what isn't good enough. He looks at you and rejoices. I believe he wants you to rejoice in his creation as well, to respond as David did—"I praise you because I am fearfully and wonderfully made; your works are wonderful; I know that full well" (Psalm 139:14). Let's pray.

Our Creator, as you made the wonderful earth and everything in it, we too are your creations. Help us to see ourselves as you see us: wonderful reflections of you. Help us to embrace our identity as your precious creations. In Jesus's name, amen.

Day Four: An Adventure in Creation

—Jewel for Your Journey—
"For we are God's handiwork, created in Christ Jesus to do good works, which God prepared in advance for us to do" (Ephesians 2:10).

I'm always up for an adventure. I love going new places, tasting new things, and seeing new sights. Whether you prefer your same walk around the park every day or would rather take a new turn down a different road, today I want you to venture out into God's creation. Don't let the summer heat of Texas or the winter wind of Minnesota stop you. Just get out in it. I have two verses I want you to meditate on while you take your journey.

Starting where we left off yesterday, Psalm 139, please read verse 16. When God formed us, he saw who we could be before we became it. Today we are going to consider who he made us to be and how to live it.

Please read Ephesians 2:8-10. The word "works" in verses 9 and 10 are the same word in Greek—*ergon*, which means toil, deed, or act. Paul is careful here to let us know that we are saved by the grace of God, not by anything we do to earn his favor. Salvation is a free gift.

Yet we were all created with purpose. According to verse 10, we were created in Christ Jesus to do good works (toil, deeds, or acts) which God prepared in advance for us to do. Looking at the original Greek, it says that we should walk in those good works. In other words, God ordained that we would do good, and created us to do it, but it's up to us to choose to walk in the purpose for which he made us.

On your adventure today, I want you to meditate and pray on what great works God prepared in advance for you to do. We are different from his other creations; we are made in his image, so we were created to create. What did he create you to create?

One last thought before you venture off: The root of the word *workmanship* is *poem*. It can also mean *fabric*. You are God's poetry, tapestry, the work of his hand. Today, ask him what he had in mind for you when he made you.

* What do you believe God created you to do?

* How can you walk in that purpose?

When we do what he designed us to do, we feel fantastically alive. Our senses are peaked, our bodies have energy to do things they wouldn't do for another purpose, and we know we are co-creating with our Creator. We feel satisfaction in our inner beings because we are doing what we were made to do. I want us to discover what that looks like—the threads of the tapestry, the woven words within us, the poem—open-ended, unfinished, but in process.

Our Father and Creator, thank you for creating us. Thank you for your grace. Thank you that even if we fall and slip and zigzag all over the road marked out for us, you still have an end in mind—that we would enter into your presence and walk in the works you made just for us to do. Help us find the pathway you carved for us and help us walk in it as we should, knowing without a doubt who we are: your daughters, your creations, designed to do good works you prepared in advance for us to do. You are amazing, and we want the amazing journey that can only be found in you. Show us God. Love, your precious creations.

Day Five: The Potter's Wheel

—Jewel for Your Journey—
*"We are the clay, you are the potter; we are all
the work of your hand" (Isaiah 64:8).*

Meet with your group and watch the video "The Second Truth: You Are a Precious Creation" at www.jenniferstrickland.net. Use the space below for notes.

Week 5 The Third Lie:

You Are What Magazines Tell You

Day One: Magazines

—Jewel for Your Journey—

"Although they claimed to be wise, they became fools and exchanged the glory of the immortal God for images made to look like a mortal human being" (Romans 1:22-23).

Today, start out by reading chapter 5.

We are certainly in the thick of it, aren't we? Looking at the messages of the fashion magazines square in the eye isn't pretty. The messages for young women have severe consequences. Making a girl feel like her face or body doesn't measure up to the standards of the culture is dangerous ground.

* As harsh as the headlines can be, it is my hope that taking a good look at the magazines will give us a deeper conviction about how to help a generation of girls bombarded with untrue messages about their value. Please take a moment to write down your insights about this chapter.

* How do you feel about the section entitled "666 Ways to Change You?" Do the messages of the magazines overwhelm you or condemn you? Or do you find them helpful? Be honest about how the titles make you feel.

* In the section "Flawed and Fabulous," I give you a list of things that *real* women *really* want. What do you really want? (If "cute buns and thighs" are on your list, there's no shame in that! Just be honest about your true desires.)

* What is your response to the section "Cosmo Speaks"?

* I enjoyed dreaming up new titles in the section "A Better Headline." What are some titles you would like to see in the magazines?

* In the section "Battle Cry," I share my heart's passion for women and girls. What is your battle cry?

Take a deep breath, sister. We are going to have some fun this week! Sometimes the best way to navigate the culture is by engaging it a little. You have another "field trip" in store on Day Four. You'll be checking out the magazine aisle in your favorite bookstore or airport or wherever you find yourself, so plan ahead! Don't worry, we won't just be looking for lies there; we will also be looking for truth. We'll be dividing the good from the bad and truth from lies. And not only will we come back with a list of false messages, but we'll also return with some good stuff: new recipes and fashion, makeup, decorating, and fitness tips too!

Father, please be with us this week. We are taking stock both of the Scriptures and the messages the world sends women and girls about their value, sexuality, and beauty. Please help us navigate these waters with the oars of truth. Love, your daughters.

Day Two: A Day of Beauty

—Jewel for Your Journey—
*"As a face is reflected in water, so the heart
reflects the real person"* (Proverbs 27:19).

Discovering the heart of beauty has been the journey of my life, and I am still discovering the meaning of authentic beauty in God's eyes. His Word is replete with messages about beauty, and we are going to focus on some precious jewels in the Word today which will illuminate our pathway to what it is to be beautiful in God's eyes.

We know that 1 Samuel 16:7 says: "People judge by outward appearance, but the Lord looks at the heart." Yes, God does focus on the heart, but we need to be honest: Man focuses on the outfit! Today, I had some pressing needs to pray about. I prayed a lot, but the truth is, I spent more time getting myself cleaned up, washing and styling my hair, and putting on my makeup and clothes than I spent on my knees! I did pray during the shower, though, and that counts!

The bottom line is, we are women, and we care about how we look. It matters to us.

* How important is your outward appearance to you? Place an X on the scale:

Not important   **Very important**

_____

* How do you think your outward appearance is a reflection of you?

Next week we are going to be studying the temple, since the Word says our bodies are God's temples. I can tell you, God isn't excited about the temple being messed up, beat up, dilapidated, dirty, and breaking down. He cares about beautifying the temple because it's a reflection of him. But more important than the outward appearance of the temple is the spirit within it. The heart of the temple is the key to its beauty.

* How important is the beauty of your heart to you? Place an X on the scale:

Not important   **Very important**

_____

* How do you think your heart is a reflection of you?

* Flip over to Proverbs 11:22. The word *discretion* in this passage means "taste, propriety, behavior, judgment, reason, understanding." How can being beautiful on the outside but lacking discretion mar our beauty?

God has a severe opinion about those who flaunt external beauty over the beauty of the heart.

* Please turn to Ezekiel 28, the prophecy of the King of Tyre, which scholars believe refers to Satan himself. Read verses 12-19.

Satan was adorned with precious stones—in fact, the king of Tyre is known to have worn bedazzled robes of priceless jewels. Yet wickedness was found in him.

* What was that wickedness (verse 17)?

As I said in the book, "Magazines distort women's worth; the devil is their partner." Satan was the original "model of perfection" whose pride and desire to be worshipped got him cast out of heaven and reduced to ashes on the ground.

Our Lord, on the other hand, is robed in kingly majesty, seated on the throne of heaven, yet he came as a man with no beauty or grandeur in his outward appearance.

* What is the difference between the beauty of Christ and the beauty of Satan?

Psalm 50:2 says, "From Zion, perfect in beauty, God shines forth." Certainly Jesus's beauty was a beauty of the heart, and it shined forth in how he loved people. It was his love that drew people to him. His love created his legacy, and the beauty of his love changes us even now.

As Galatians 5:6 says, "The only thing that counts is faith expressing itself through love." The legacy of our beauty too begins in our hearts and spills out through love.

 * Let's close today's study by looking at Philippians 2:1-11. If Jesus was the manifestation of a God "perfect in beauty," then what characteristics do you think God considers beautiful?

I find it fascinating that as Satan desired to exalt himself on account of his physical beauty, God reduced him to eating ashes on the ground like a slithering snake. But as Christ gave up the throne of heaven to be a servant, healer, teacher, and lover of souls, God exalted him to the highest place and gave him the name that is above every name, that at the name of Jesus every knee should bow.

I look forward to exploring the beauty of God with you further tomorrow as we look into the topic of fashion!

Father, help us to imitate Christ, the author and perfecter of real beauty. In his name, amen.

Day Three: The Fashionista

—Jewel for Your Journey—
*"Let the king be enthralled by your beauty; honor
him, for he is your lord" (Psalm 45:11).*

Just because I was a model doesn't mean I know all that much about fashion. It's really not my gift. Going to the mall is completely overwhelming for me. I'd rather be in a small boutique than wandering through a gazillion racks of clothes. And I can't do it without a good friend telling me what to try on and what to take off!

Some of my best friends are fashionistas, and they've helped me out on more than one occasion. I have girlfriends who are makeup artists and hairstylists, who also see their gifts as ministry to others. Who doesn't love a makeover, especially when it's with someone who also prays for you? It's amazing how fresh makeup, a new haircut, a great outfit, and a word of encouragement help us feel better about ourselves.

Yet as we read yesterday, pride on account of our external appearance doesn't please God. He is not opposed to beauty; rather, he is the author of it, and most references to beauty in the Old Testament describe women. There was one group of women, however, who greatly displeased God because they put their stock in external adornments instead of in him. They are the women of Zion.

* Please read Isaiah 3:16. How does the Lord describe these women?

* Keep reading verses 17-26. What does the Lord do to them?

Because The Message version puts words into pictures for us, read the passage here in this translation:

> God say, "Zion women are stuck-up, prancing around
> in their high heels,
>
> Making eyes at all the men in the street, swinging their
> hips,

Tossing their hair, gaudy and garish in cheap jewelry."

The Master will fix it so those Zion women will all turn bald—

Scabby, bald-headed women.

The Master will do it.

The time is coming when the Master will strip them of their fancy baubles—the dangling earrings, anklets and bracelets, combs and mirrors and silk scarves, diamond brooches and pearl necklaces, the rings on their fingers and the rings on their toes, the latest fashions in hats, exotic perfumes and aphrodisiacs, gowns and capes, all the world's finest in fabrics and design.

Instead of wearing seductive scents, these women are going to smell like rotting cabbages;

Instead of modeling flowing gowns, they'll be sporting rags;

Instead of their stylish hairdos, scruffy heads;

Instead of beauty marks, scabs and scars (Isaiah 3:16-24).

The women of Zion went from tramping about, flaunting their embellishments, to being bald, wearing sackcloth, and sitting on the ground, destitute—not a far cry from what God did to oppose the pride of Satan. But the Lord is not done with his women yet; he does not banish them forever. Once he has taken away their favorite things, they will see what beauty is and where their security lies.

Flip to chapter 4 and read verses 2-6. Here is The Message version of Zion's restoration:

> "GOD will give Zion's women a good bath. He'll scrub
> the bloodstained city of its violence and brutality, purge
> the place with a firestorm of judgment.

Then GOD will bring back the ancient pillar of cloud
by day and the pillar of fire by night and mark Mount
Zion and everyone in it with his glorious presence, his
immense, protective presence, shade from the burning
sun and shelter from the driving rain" (Isaiah 4:4-6).

When we are humbled, the scales fall off our eyes and we realize
it's not all about us. We see what is really beautiful—the Branch of
the Lord, Christ. God washes away the filth of the women of Zion,
forgiving their sin and cleansing their bloodstains. Then his presence hovers over them, his glory like a canopy, "a shelter and shade
from the heat of the day, and a refuge and hiding place from the
storm and the rain."

* What was the Lord opposed to with the women of Zion? What
did he want to show them?

Our Lord is not angry with purses and mirrors; he's angry at
pride. Sometimes he takes everything away from us so we can see
what is truly precious—his presence in our lives and his love hovering over us. Eventually the Lord restores the women of Zion to
their state of beauty, but I bet they were never the same after being
humbled by him.

* Please turn to Psalm 45:3-9. Believed to have been written for
the marriage of King Solomon, this messianic psalm prophetically pictures the marriage between Christ and his church. Note
the adornments of the groom (verse 3-6). What fashion statement does he make?

We do believe in a God of fairy tales, don't we? I picture him riding on a horse victoriously, with truth, humility, and righteousness in his stride. He is dressed in splendor and majesty, returning for his bride.

* Read verses 10-15. How does the groom see his bride (verse 11)?

* What do her adornments represent?

This verse is our jewel for today's journey. He loves the beauty of the woman—he is enthralled with it—yet she is not adorned just with a great dress, but with joy and gladness. There is such purity in her; there is no pride in this bride. She completely honors her groom, and that's what's beautiful about her.

At one time in my life, I was so full of pride, and he humbled me. He took away my externals to show me himself. He cleansed me and dressed me in garments of salvation, and now he says to me—and to you—"the king is enthralled with your beauty. Honor him, for he is your lord." The woman who looks at him with honor is the woman who is beautiful to him, and his love further beautifies her.

* Please read Song of Songs 4:1-10. God loves the beauty of the woman. He fashioned it and he adores it. Write down verse 7 to remember how he sees you:

* How does that verse make you feel?

* What is his greatest delight (verse 10)?

A beautiful woman dresses herself in *him*. She "[clothes herself] with the Lord Jesus Christ" (Romans 13:14).

* She dresses herself in purity, honor, and reverence for her king. What would it look like for you to dress yourself beautifully in his eyes, so that he would be "enthralled with your beauty"?

Let's close in prayer.

Lord, you are our King, and someday we want to see you in all your beauty and reflect that beauty back to you. Thank you that you wash our torn and soiled clothes and turn them into garments of salvation and praise. May we see ourselves and even the clothes we wear the way you see them. Help us to remember, as you said to the little girl turned queen in Ezekiel 16:14, that the splendor you give us makes our beauty perfect. Amen.

Day Four: A Trip to the Bookstore

—Jewel for Your Journey—

"Dear friends, do not believe every spirit, but test the spirits to see whether they are from God" (1 John 4:1).

Can we please have some fun today? All this talk about fashion is making me want to shop, or at least go buy some new perfume! We'll do some shopping next week, but today we are putting the brakes on Bible study and heading to the bookstore.

The plan is to grab a friend or daughter, get your favorite drink, and peruse the best magazine racks you can find. We are going to practice being able to rightly divide good from bad; truth from lies. If you feel like you already know how to do that, I hope you'll bring a younger woman along whom you can teach.

Keep in mind that we aren't just looking for lies on the magazine racks; we are also looking for truth. The Bible says to "test everything that is said. Hold on to what is good" (1 Thessalonians 5:21 NLT). So look for some great recipes while you are there or brush up on what you enjoy—working out, decorating, cooking, cleaning tips, building a business, athletics…whatever you find that is good for you, hold on to it and plan to bring it back to your group to share.

To arm ourselves, let's read 1 John 4:1-6. As verse 4 says, the one who is in you is greater than the one who is in the world. The one who is in you is Christ, and Christ can distinguish truth from lies. Ask the Holy Spirit to help you discern the viewpoint of the world from what is in line with God's viewpoint.

We have deeper convictions about truth when we have deeper convictions about lies. I have created a chart for you to fill in while you are checking out the magazines. Fill it up with headlines, articles, and descriptions of images. You may not want to purchase magazines but you do want to share their concepts with your group for tomorrow's meeting. So write them down.

Truths (Good Messages)   **Lies (Wrong Messages)**

I hope you come back with some new recipes for your girlfriends. Or at least some good info on skin care or managing money. But I also hope you are bold enough to go face-to-face with the lies you see in the fashion and beauty magazines and share those lies with others.

Day Five: Beautiful To Me

—Jewel for Your Journey—
*"Why are you bothering this woman? She has done
a beautiful thing to me" (Matthew 26:10).*

Meet with your group and watch the video "The Third Lie: You Are What Magazines Tell You" at www.jenniferstrickland .net. Use the space below for notes.

Week 6 The Third Truth:

You Are a Beautiful Temple

Day One: Holy

— Jewel for Your Journey —

*"The body...is not meant for sexual immorality but for the
Lord, and the Lord for the body" (1 Corinthians 6:13).*

Read chapter 6. What stood out to you most from this chapter?

* Respond to this statement, describing the messages of the magazines: "Your body is a toy. Sex is a game. Have at it, baby girl."

* What do you think is the impact of political correctness on the younger generation's view of their sexuality?

✻ When you hear, "Your body is a temple," what does that stir up in you?

✻ How can you be a "temple gate called Beautiful"?

Day Two: The Adulterous Bride

—Jewel for Your Journey—
*"Unbelievable! How could such a thing
ever happen?" (Ezekiel 16:16 NLT).*

My friend, I am not unaware of the sensitivity of the material we are studying today. Tackling these subjects can be tough to say the least, but I believe the church has to address the deepest issues affecting God's children. The Word does not shy away from saying it like it is, so we shouldn't either.

Let's open this day with prayer and trust God will only take us where he wants us to go.

Dear Lord, when we talk about our bodies, we have to look at sin and how it affects us, bodily, emotionally, and spiritually. Help us navigate dicey waters with your Word as our guide. Help us to open our hearts this week to whatever you have for us. Teach us what it means to be holy, to be a temple, to be beautiful in your eyes. In Jesus's precious name, amen.

One time I was praying in preparation for giving the "temple" message at an upcoming retreat. As I was praying, I felt the Lord say, *Yes, let's work on the temple—your temple.* And in that moment, he brought things to my mind and heart that needed to be cleared out of my temple—things like anger, unforgiveness, and bitterness. I was able to confess those things to him and allowed him to "clean house," making me a better vessel for his Spirit. There have been many times when the Lord and I have done some serious one-on-one cleaning in the temple of me.

Part of our journey together this week is going to be studying the body as a temple; other portions will be allowing him to bring to light any sin lingering in our temples which may be preventing us from experiencing the peace and joy of Christ.

God hates sin in the temple. The reason he hates it is because it hurts us. He is feverishly passionate about his daughters, and when we fall prey to temptation and give full birth to sin, his Spirit rises up and says, "This shall not be in my Father's house!"

We are going to start our day of study by revisiting our baby girl turned queen of Ezekiel 16. Remember that the story of the girl is symbolic of Jerusalem, God's dearly loved people, whom he had rescued and restored and who later turned to idols and sin before they came back to him. I wish I could say our baby girl remained faithful to her Maker, but she didn't.

Please read Ezekiel 16:1-3, to understand our context. Jerusalem's ancestry was pagan, and here God is letting his people know that adopting their ancestors' detestable practices is unacceptable to him. In verses 4-14 we are told the story of how he redeemed the broken Jerusalem with his love. We know he adorned her with fine clothing and expensive jewelry and gave her choice food to eat. She became very beautiful and rose to be a queen, famous among the nations, and the splendor God gave her made her beauty perfect.

* Please read the unfolding of her story in Ezekiel 16:15-22. Where did her sin begin? What did she trust in (verse 15)?

* What choices did she make with her adornments?

Her adornments symbolized her worth to God; they were objects of his affection and representative of her salvation, redemption, renewed righteousness, and authority. But like the women of Zion (and Satan himself), she became proud on account of her beauty and lavished her favors on other lovers. She turned to other nations and their false gods instead of staying true to her Redeemer.

* What does she do to her children?

Child sacrifice became a common practice, and because of such vile acts among the people and priesthood, the temple became unfit for God to inhabit. He left the temple, no longer serving as the people's guide and protector.

* Continue reading verses 23-34. How did she degrade her beauty (verse 25)?

You know, I want to call up *Cosmopolitan* now and let them know that a woman's beauty is degraded when she gives herself away sexually—and that increasing promiscuity leads to the sacrifice of unborn children, which breaks the heart of God and leaves the woman feeling insatiably thirsty for something more satisfying to fill her.

* Fill in the blank from verses 28-29: Sexual sin leaves us feeling
_____.

One of the things the fashion and beauty magazines don't mention to young women is that no matter how many lovers they have or how much sex they have, they will not feel fulfilled. In addition, they will suffer the consequence. In the case of Jerusalem, God reduced her territory and eventually allows the whole city to collapse.

* What is the Lord so angry about in verses 31-34?

God's anger burns against Jerusalem, his "adulterous wife," because she gives herself away for free, as if neither she nor her husband is worth payment. I cannot help but apply this truth to women and girls today, who give their bodies away as if they have no value and their future husbands are not worth waiting for. I know what this is, and I know what the consequences are. When I "wed" Christ, I became a renewed virgin and waited for my husband. Yet to this day I regret ever giving away my body before marriage; it had consequences I'd rather live without. At the time, I simply did not know my value, my future husband's true worth, and the holiness of the marriage bed. Today, I know the weight of their glory as fine gold.

Continue reading verses 35-42, remembering this is not an actual woman; this is an allegory wherein God is comparing his bride, his people, to an adulterous and murderous wife.

* How does God feel about sexual promiscuity?

* How does God feel about adultery?

✳ How does God feel about the sacrifice of children?

 We serve a jealous God. He is jealous for us. He wants us all
to himself; he weeps when we pour ourselves into "other lovers."
He also makes a great assertion in this passage—one sin leads to
another. First, pride in beauty; second, sexual sin; third, murder;
fourth, alienation from God. His Spirit cannot be in the presence
of such sin.

 The only reason I can still breathe after reading this passage
is because I know his tremendous redemption. "Then my wrath
against you will subside and my jealous anger will turn away from
you; I will be calm and no longer angry" (Ezekiel 16:42). Thank
God we aren't stoned anymore for our sin; thank God we aren't
hacked with whips and cords. He sent his son to take the stripes for
our fallenness.

 Please take a moment to go deeper by reading Jeremiah 32:30-
41. After the destruction of Jerusalem, God calls his people back as
his bride. No matter how much evil we have done, he still wants to
marry us.

 When we are unfaithful, he is faithful. When we break our promises, he keeps his! It breaks his heart when we turn our backs, but
he still wants us.

 The Lord told our baby girl turned queen in Ezekiel 16, "I will
remember the covenant I made with you in the days of your youth,
and I will establish an everlasting covenant with you....I [will] make
atonement for you for all you have done" (verses 60, 63).

✳ Please read 1 Corinthians 6:18-20 and fill in the blank: Your body
   is a _____ of the _____; You are not your
   own; you were _____ at a price.

* What is the price for which you were bought?

* As a result, what are we to do with our bodies?

* Why are we to "flee" from sexual immorality (verse 18)?

Reading The Message version helps us see familiar Scripture in a new light. Check out these powerful words on the body and sex as they relate to Christ:

> God honored the Master's body by raising it from the grave. He'll treat yours with the same resurrection power. Until that time, remember that your bodies are created with the same dignity as the Master's body. You wouldn't take the Master's body off to a whorehouse, would you? I should hope not. There's more to sex than mere skin on skin. Sex is as much spiritual mystery as physical fact. As written in Scripture, "The two become one." Since we want to become spiritually one with the Master, we must not pursue the kind of sex that avoids commitment and intimacy, leaving us more lonely than ever—the kind of sex that can never "become one." There is a sense in which sexual sins are different from all others. In sexual sin we violate the sacredness of our own bodies, these bodies that were made for God-given and God-modeled love, for "becoming one" with another.

Or didn't you realize that your body is a sacred place, the place of the Holy Spirit? Don't you see that you can't live however you please, squandering what God paid such a high price for? The physical part of you is not some piece of property belonging to the spiritual part of you. God owns the whole works. So let people see God in and through your body (1 Corinthians 6:14-20 MSG).

* Please read 1 Thessalonians 4:3-8. What is the key to avoiding sexual immorality (verse 4)?

* What kind of life does God call us to live (verse 7)?

* Let's wrap up this day of study with a refreshing look at Jesus and the woman caught in adultery. These eight brief verses show us how our Lord sees us and deals with our sin. Please turn to the book of John and read 8:1-8. Knowing how passionate God is about faithfulness, what does this passage tell you about our Lord?

* What does he tell the woman? How does he deal with those who are eager to pass judgment on her?

* Following his example, how are we supposed to deal with women whose lives have been riddled by sexual sin?

There is no condemnation for any who are in Christ; he is compassionate, merciful, and forgiving. He rises up to defend his daughters because he loves us with an everlasting love, no matter what poor choices we have made. Yet, he speaks to us: "Go now, and leave your life of sin."

Lord, I don't just want us to call you Lord. I want you to be our Lord. Lord of the temples of us, our bodies' sacred ground. Forgive us and cleanse us by the power of your blood from any unrighteousness in our bodies and sexuality. Forgive us, Jesus, and help us to sin no more. Give us a new heart and a new spirit so that we can teach our daughters, the next generation of women and girls, to save themselves for you, faithfully consecrated and committed to walk as your pure and radiant bride. In Jesus's name, amen.

Day Three: The Temple of You

— Jewel for Your Journey —
"Yet you desired faithfulness even in the womb; you taught me wisdom in that secret place" (Psalm 51:6).

As women, we do a lot of cleaning house. We organize drawers and closets, scrub carpets and mop floors, clean mirrors and polish countertops, wash dishes and clean out the refrigerator. The fun part is choosing paint colors, hanging décor, selecting attractive fabrics, and positioning accessories. Why do we do all this? Because it's our home. We want to create an inviting space where family and friends can relax and feel cared for.

We also keep our homes nice for ourselves. We live there, so we want our home to be an orderly, clean, and friendly environment. We wouldn't let just anyone come into our home, make a mess of things, and steal from us, leaving us violated. We create boundaries around our home to protect it. So it is with our bodies. They should not be treated as trash heaps or motels where people can just stay the night and go on their merry way, leaving us to deal with the mess. Our bodies are God's house, and he cares about what goes on inside of us.

* Please begin by reading John 14:23. What does Jesus say he and the Father will do if we obey his teaching?

When we start looking at our bodies as Christ's home, I believe we treat it differently and become more attuned to things he wants us to change. One thing God cannot coexist with is sin. That is why he tells the forgiven woman, "Go and sin no more." Forgiveness is not permission for her to continue in her licentious lifestyle, because that will only harm her.

Paul often addressed sexual sin in the church because people battled with it, but he didn't limit his discussion of sin to immorality. Aware that we struggle with godlessness in many forms, Paul addressed them all.

It was shortly after I became a Christian that some women showed me a few of these verses, and for the first time in my life I became aware of what sin was. Sometimes we think of sin as something "bad people" do, but I've always found it fascinating that immorality is listed right next to greed and selfishness. In reviewing these verses we can rejoice in how the Spirit has transformed us from our old lives and ask him to help us see ways we still need to shed that old skin and adorn ourselves with the life of Christ.

Please read the following verses and list here the sins Paul is concerned about in the church:

* 1 Corinthians 6:9-11:

* 2 Corinthians 12:20-21:

* Galatians 5:19-21:

* Leave a bookmark in Galatians because we will be returning to it. Turn to Romans 6:1-4 and 11-14. How does Paul describe our relationship to sin?

* How does our baptism represent our relationship to sin?

* Instead of offering the parts of our body to sin, what are we supposed to offer our body to?

* How can you do that on a practical level? Give an example.

* Please continue reading verses 15-23. Is there any sin in your life that you feel like you are still a slave to? How can you make the choice to live free of that sin?

* Offering ourselves as "slaves to righteousness" leads to what? Circle one:

forgiveness   impurity   holiness

This is what I know: Without the righteousness of Christ, we are dead in our sins. Holiness is a work of the Holy Spirit, not a work of the flesh. No matter how hard we try we will always fall short. But when we submit ourselves to the work of the Holy Spirit within us, we become clearer reflections of a holy God.

If we are in Christ, we have been set free from sin and will not pay its death penalty. Yet if he reveals a hindrance to his work in our lives, it may be time to get real about it, be truthful, and carry the weight of that stumbling block to the altar so that we can be released from its burden.

* Please read Psalm 51:1-17, out loud if you can. Write verse 17 here:

* How does this passage speak to you today?

Tomorrow I am going to give you a chance to let the Holy Spirit do some temple-cleaning with you. So plan to get out of the house, take a walk, or spend some time in prayer in a private place. But for today, we are going to continue with some wonderful reading.

* Please read Colossians 2:13-15. What did Christ do on the cross for us?

These are precious words. Please understand, he remembers your sin no more. So looking at what sin is today doesn't mean it's being held against us. It could, however, be holding us back. Since we are his house, he may want to clean up a little…or a lot!

Continue reading Colossians 3:1-18. When I get new clothes, it's hard to just sift them in with the old clothes. I like them to have their own special spot. Better yet, I get rid of some old raggedy things to make room for the new. While the magazines focus on clothes as a matter of fashion, biblically, clothing is symbolic for much more. When we come to Christ, we shed the old grave clothes and receive the new. There may be some old habits we need to toss in the trash like tattered rags.

On the left-hand column, list the practices of the old self from verses 5-9. On the right-hand column, list the new clothes of the Christ follower from verses 12-17.

Old Clothes   **New Clothes**

I don't know about you, but I just discovered some old clothes in my closet that really don't look good on me, and I'm tossing them in the trash. As Paul says, we died to sin. How can we live in it any longer? As the Lord said to his people at the very beginning of the book of Isaiah, before he called them on the carpet about their sin: "Though your sins are like scarlet, they shall be as white as snow; though they are red as crimson, they shall be like wool" (1:18). We are justified freely by his grace. Yet he still wants to cut off any branch in us that bears no fruit, and sin only bears fruit for death.

There has not been a season in my Christian life when I haven't needed to come before the Lord and confess sin. The first thing we have to do is agree with him that our sin is actually sin, and that it is holding us back from the freedom, fullness, and possible destiny he has for us. His ultimate goal is to transform us to be more like him. So if anything today has come up in your heart—whether it's judging others or hatred or self-centeredness or sexual sin or greed or envy—I want you to close this day by giving those things to the Lord and asking for his forgiveness and transformation.

Remember, when we take off the old outfit, he wants to adorn us with a new one. So as you "turn in" your old clothes that will be turned to dust, ask him to dress you in a new garment that gives you lasting beauty. For example, you might say, "Lord, today I am turning in my rage; please dress me in a garment of gentleness and patience."

✳ Lord, today I am turning in my _____.

✳ Please dress me in a garment of _____.

Lord, help us to rid ourselves of the grave clothes. Help us to bury that old self with you and be raised in new life. Clothe us, Lord, with your favorite outfit for us: compassion, kindness, humility, gentleness, and patience. Help us to forgive as you have forgiven us. Overall, help us to wear love as our most beautiful and precious garment. Give us power

*over sin as we hereby ask and allow the Holy Spirit to reign supreme
within us. Make us into the beautiful temples you designed us to be.*

Day Four: Inside Out

—Jewel for Your Journey—
*"First clean the inside of the cup and dish, and then
the outside also will be clean" (Matthew 23:26).*

To close out this week, I want you to do something special for
your temple. I want you to give it a good cleaning, inside and
out. Jesus has strong words for those who make over the outside
but fail to clean the inside. We are going to read a few short verses
today and then I'm sending you on your way to do some temple
work of your own!

* Read Matthew 15:17-20, taking a close look at the things Jesus
lists that make us unclean. Is there anything in your heart that is
causing you to be unclean? Explain.

* Read Jesus's powerful words to the Pharisees in Matthew 23:25-
28. What is he saying about cleaning the outside of the cup and
dish and not the inside?

The world tells us to have a makeover from the outside in, claiming this will change us to be more beautiful. But God beautifies us
from the inside out. Today I want you to spend some time alone
with the Lord, Grab your journal, Bible, or some good walking

shoes, and steal some precious time with him. Ask him, "Lord, what do you want to cleanse from the temple of me?" Be truthful about any gunk that has been lining the inward parts of your heart. Lay it before him, confessing, repenting, and possibly grieving the impact that sin has had on you and others. Receive his mercy for you. Then ask him what new clothes he has for you to wear. What beautiful garment does he want to replace with the one that diminishes your beauty? Maybe it's praise and prayer in place of division and despair; maybe it's joy in place of worry; faith in place of fear. Maybe it's victory over the victim-mentality, or kindness instead of cruelty. Maybe it's service over selfishness. Ask him, and you will receive your answer.

When you are done with your interior temple-cleaning, go and clean the outside of your cup. This week, treat yourself to a haircut, a facial, a mani/pedi, a new lip color, or a new top. Ask him to dress you with himself, making you continually more beautiful as you reflect him more and more.

Day Five: The Temple Clearing

— Jewel for Your Journey —
"When all the people saw him walking and praising God, they recognized him as the same man who used to sit begging at the temple gate called Beautiful" (Acts 3:9-10).

Meet with your group and watch the video "The Third Truth: You Are a Beautiful Temple" at www.jenniferstrickland.net. Use the space below for notes.

Week 7 The Fourth Lie:

You Are the Mask You Wear

Day One: Taking Off the Mask

—Jewel for Your Journey—
*"Satan himself masquerades as an angel
of light" (2 Corinthians 11:14).*

Read chapter 7 and contemplate these questions with me:
Why do we wear masks?

* What happens when women and girls wear masks that disguise
their pain?

* What kind of masks do you wear?

✳ What would "unmasking" look like for you?

This week your "field trip" assignment will be to talk to another woman about what is beneath your mask. Choose that woman wisely; plan ahead. Whether it is a best friend, a mentor, a counselor, or someone you believe can speak wisdom into your life or situation, please pray about the right person and trust God will lead you to her. Plan for coffee, a scheduled phone call, lunch, or (best yet) a sleepover!

If, on the other hand, you feel like you have done your share of receiving mentoring, counseling, and advice, and you have spent a lot of time looking at what's beneath the surface of your heart and allowing other women to help you get to the bottom of it, then I would like to offer an alternate assignment: Go face-to-face with a hurting woman or girl. I bet you know someone who would love some special time with you, someone who would love to tell you how life is going beneath the surface. Pray about who, what, when, where, and why—God will answer.

This is going to be a great week of study. We are going deep! Prepare your heart!

Day Two: Unveiled

—Jewel for Your Journey—
*"But whenever anyone turns to the Lord, the
veil is taken away" (2 Corinthians 3:16).*

Making things look good on the surface is highly exalted in our culture. Culturally, a healthy relationship with God and each other is not as important as a good-looking image. But God sees the heart, and he wants to get beyond the exterior and transform our interior. He is more interested in us being healed on the inside than looking proper on the outside. The question is, what does he want to do with our insides, and how do we become less a reflection of the culture and more a reflection of him?

It all starts with turning away from the values of the culture and turning to him for our reflection. But when we come before him, there are no masks allowed. No cover-ups. No veils.

Before Christ, there was a veil in the temple, separating the Holy Place from the Most Holy Place. The high priest was the only one who could cross the veil into the Most Holy Place, once a year, to make a sacrifice for the people's sins. When Christ died on the cross, however, that veil was torn in two. No longer does our sin separate us from a holy God. Through faith in Christ, we can now enter his presence—the Most Holy Place—freely and confidently.

In the passage you are about to read, Paul is describing God's delivery of the Ten Commandments to Moses on Mount Sinai. On the mountain, Moses went face-to-face with God, and the impact was so profound that when Moses came down the mountain, his face reflected the intense radiance of God's glory. To keep the Israelites from being shocked by his shining countenance, Moses wore a veil over his face.

In our passage today, Paul is telling the Corinthians that trying to obey the Ten Commandments led to death, because no one could ever do so perfectly. Yet even the delivery of the law on tablets of stone was exacted with glory. How much more glorious, Paul argues, is the delivery of the Spirit which brings life. The life of the Spirit is written not on stone but on hearts, making us more and more glorious as the Spirit transforms us to be like Christ.

Please read 2 Corinthians 3:7-11. Note that the radiance of Moses's face faded away over time; but the radiance of the Spirit is *lasting*.

Continue reading verses 12-18. The veil Paul is speaking of not only represents the physical veil Moses wore, but also the spiritual veil that covers people's hearts and minds. This veil represents

a hardness of heart that prevents us from being penetrated by the
ministry of Christ.

* Scripture says there is only one way the veil can be removed.
  What is it?

Continue reading 2 Corinthians 3:16-18. Let's read The Message
version of verses 16-18:

> Whenever, though, they turn to face God as Moses did,
> God removes the veil and there they are—face to face!
> They suddenly recognize that God is a living, personal
> presence, not a piece of chiseled stone. And when God is
> personally present, a living Spirit, that old, constricting
> legislation is recognized as obsolete. We're free of it! All
> of us! Nothing between us and God, our faces shining
> with the brightness of his face. And so we are transfig-
> ured much like the Messiah, our lives gradually becom-
> ing brighter and more beautiful as God enters our lives
> and we become like him.

* What is the freedom we have been granted through the cross?

* What happens when the veil is removed between us and God?

In Christ, we can enter into his presence without the veil and
go face-to-face with God. When we do that, we are transformed to

be more like him. The original Greek word translated as *reflected* actually means "beholding as in a glass," or "to mirror oneself." In other words, when we are bare before him, he can work with that! The Spirit can transform us to reflect his beauty from the inside out.

Something key to understand here is that there is no shame. No matter where we have been or what's been done to us, we can approach him with freedom and confidence. As Psalm 34:5 says, "Those that look to him are radiant; their faces are never covered with shame."

∗ Turn now to Hebrews 12:1-2. Who are we to fix our eyes on?

∗ What do we need to "throw off" and why?

∗ Who are we to fix our eyes on?

∗ Why did he endure the cross?

There just is no shame left for us. He bore it all. When God allowed sin to tear the body of Christ, he tore down the veil. He removed the separation between us and himself.

We are going to close this day of study with powerful words from Romans 8:29-38. Ask God to help you unpack it with the following prompts.

* What does verse 28 promise us?

* From verse 29, what did he predestine you to be conformed to?

* What can separate you from the love of Christ?

* In light of this, do you feel you can approach God as you are, unmasked? Why or why not?

* Let's close this day with an exercise in unmasking. Please use the space below to write what's on your unveiled heart:

* If you sense the Spirit speaking anything to you in response to what you've shared, please write it here:

* How can you live the truths we've looked at today?

My friend, you and I are free. Free from masks and free from veils. Free to approach him face-to-face. Let's pray.

Lord, please help us approach you face-to-face, where real transformation begins. Help us to know that there, in the Most Holy Place, your love surrounds us. Change us, Holy Spirit, to be better reflections of your faith, your hope, and your love. In Jesus's name, amen.

Day Three: The Worship of Image

— Jewel for Your Journey —

"How you have fallen from heaven, morning star, son of the dawn!" (Isaiah 14:12).

I want us to get some serious conviction about the dangers of worshipping image over truth. We were made in God's image; therefore his desire is to reflect his image through us. But without even realizing it, we can begin to look to the world for our affirmation. Instead of looking to God, we look to others. Instead of seeing ourselves in the mirror of his Word, we see ourselves in the bathroom mirror. We focus on the image of the stars in magazines and movies and television. Without thought, we applaud the images of glamorous people whose personal lives are falling apart, forgetting that real beauty is found at home. We get starstruck.

Women and girls who take great care to perfect their exterior while shutting God out of their interior end up confused. We look to the god of Facebook and Instagram to tell us we are approved of; we hope a new profile picture will get us more "likes." Yet all the while, God is waiting in the interior room of the temple, hoping we will come behind the curtain. In this Most Holy Place, the private corridor of our hearts, he waits.

We are going to start our study today by reminding ourselves of the mastermind of image-worship, the enemy of our souls, Satan.

✻ Please read 2 Corinthians 11:14. What does this verse tell you about Satan?

Please remember that Satan masqueraded as a truth-teller in the Garden of Eden. He assured Eve she need not heed God's commands, convincing her that separation from her husband and the will of God was good. And what did he use to tempt her? A tree, "pleasing to the eye" and satisfying to the flesh, that would exalt her to a god-like state. It was pretty, it would feel good, and it would make her wise like God.

✻ Please revisit Ezekiel 28, the prophecy of Satan as he is likened to the King of Tyre. Read verses 1-18. What was Satan's perception of himself?

✻ What was he proud about?

✻ What was God opposed to in Satan and what did he do about it?

* Read verses 11-19. How was Satan the king of the masquerade?

* Describe his fate.

* How does God feel about pride in external wealth, wisdom, and beauty?

* Please turn now to Isaiah's prophesy about the king of Babylon, likening him to Satan in Isaiah 14:3-15. What is Satan called in verse 12?

Everything Satan represents is a copycat of the real thing. Everything that Christ is—authentic, pure, and true—Satan copycats, but he is a fake.

* Turn now to Revelation 22:16 and write here what Jesus's name is—don't forget the capital letters!

Don't you love a Lord who is the light of all creation, who lowered himself to come to earth as base as a baby in a manger, with no room for him in the inn? A Savior who was willing to do a carpenter's labor although he crafted the earth? A King who wore a crown of all our pain to show the lavishness of his love? How opposite from the enemy! How opposite a mask-wearer, a fake, and a pompous liar posing as a god!

We must know who we are dealing with when it comes to the worship of wealth, wisdom, and beauty over service, humility, and sacrifice. Since Jesus is highly exalted over an already-defeated enemy, let's turn our attention to Christ for a picture of the kind of image that glorifies God instead of self.

In the book of John 12:1-8, we read that Jesus passes through Bethany six days before the Passover. Mary anoints him for his burial, while Judas, the mask-wearer, accuses her of wasting money. Jesus defends her because her humility, sacrifice, and offering is beautiful to him; she is a living rejection of Satan. In the next several passages, he explains his death and summarizes his message.

* Read John 12:23-26. Most people think to be glorified, we must be exalted. Jesus teaches the opposite. How does he say he will be glorified?

* What does dying to self result in?

* Fill in the blank: "My father will honor the one who _____ me."

* Continue reading verses 27-36. Who is the prince of this world?

* What will drive him out?

* What do you think it means to be "children of light" (verse 36)?

* Read verses 37-43. Why did the people not believe him? Circle all that apply:

Satan had blinded their eyes and deadened their hearts.

They would not turn to him.

They loved praise from men more than praise from God.

All of the above.

* Read verses 44-45 and fill in the blank. "The one who looks at me is seeing _____."

That's awesome to me. Jesus goes on to declare, "I have come into the world as a light, so that no one who believes in me should stay in darkness." Have you ever thought about how dark it is behind a mask? How obscured our vision? How separated we are?

Jesus was never afraid to go face-to-face with people. He preferred people unmasked, and still does. He was intimately connected to people during his time on earth, and we can still have that face-to-face intimacy with him now. When we see him, we see God, and God is light. Let's step into the light and follow him. Let's refuse darkness. Let's agree with him that as we humble ourselves as servants, we too will be lifted up.

Please close this day with prayer.

Day Four: Come to the Mountain

—Jewel for Your Journey—

*"There he was transfigured before them. His
face shone like the sun, and his clothes became
as white as the light" (Matthew 17:2).*

Today is "field trip" day. I hope you've made plans to talk to a friend or give another woman or girl the gift of your time. I'd like you to read two passages of Scripture to set the tone for your time together.

* Read Luke 9:28-36, the Transfiguration. What happens to Jesus in this scene?

When Jesus brings his three friends up to the mountain to pray, he shows them who he really is. He shows them his true identity, and his glory literally radiates from the inside out. He trusted *three* of them. He didn't become completely "unveiled" in front of crowds on the hilltops. He trusted a select few before whom he could peel back the layers and show his true nature. On the mountain, they met up with a couple of friends who already knew who Jesus was, Moses and Elijah, which makes a group of six. Here we have our first "small group."

We all need a Peter, James, and John in our lives—people who are following God but not quite sure about the setup, the destination, and the future. They are co-travelers who can experience the exchange of companionship, friendship, and wisdom. And we all need a Moses and Elijah, people who are ahead of us on the road of life, who can smile at the future and speak truth to us when our heads get duped by beautiful lies.

My deepest transformation has been in baring my heart to God when I am alone, and baring my heart unmasked to women who will pray with me and not judge me. This is why both your group experience and your face-to-face time is so important. If even Jesus shared who he really was beneath the surface with a handful of trusted people, then we need that too.

* Turn to Matthew 18:20 and write it here:

In the face-to-face and in the group experience, he is there and he will speak to us.

Remember that after the Transfiguration, Jesus's trusted friends told *no one* what they saw. As true friends in search of God's voice, we must maintain an environment of security. Anything you or anyone in your face-to-face time shares is completely confidential. Don't go running down the mountain to blab another's confessions. In this journey, we are trusting one another to pray, to hear from God, and to usher us along that all-important transformative journey where we become more like Christ.

Lord, you are the light. In you there is no darkness at all. During our special time with a woman or girl whom you have chosen for us this week, please help us be unmasked. As we come together, help us talk heart to heart. Thank you for being there with us. On the mountain, the Spirit of the Lord grants us freedom to be forthcoming about the areas in our hearts you want us to change. Allow us to help guide each other on the illuminated path. In Jesus's name, amen.

Day Five: Face to Face

—Jewel for Your Journey—
"Why are you bothering this woman? She has done a beautiful thing to me" (Matthew 26:10).

Meet with your group and watch the video "The Fourth Lie: You Are the Mask You Wear" at www.jenniferstrickland.net. Use the space below for notes.

Week 8   The Fourth Truth:

You Are a Shining Light

Day One: Wives

— Jewel for Your Journey —

"Wives, submit yourselves to your own husbands
as you do to the Lord" (Ephesians 5:22).

Read Chapter 8. While the women's rights movement gave women the freedom to manifest their gifts outside the home, it also had a backlash: Women began to believe a lie. "You don't need a man" to have a baby, launch a career, or get your desires met. Life outside the home trumped life inside; and children and marriages suffered. This insidious lie has corrupted more marriages than we can count. Men have been trampled upon and disrespected, and God's order is not honored. His Spirit does not reign in homes where there is dishonor, discord, dissension, and disrespect. "A house divided against itself will fall," the Word tells us (Luke 11:17).

The secular media is of no help. Divorce, adultery, sexual communion with men, women, or both, is exalted and presented as attractive. When women in Hollywood are applauded for their achievements outside the home, no one seems to grieve their fallen families. There is no movement toward God's design for marriage coming from the world.

Instead, the world applauds the exterior, saying, "Image is everything." According to the world, it's more important for a woman to look good outside the house than to be good within it. But you and I know we are made in God's image and designed to reflect his image, and Jesus reflected the same love in his face-to-face interactions as he did to the masses. In fact, if you study his one-on-one encounters with people, you might find he was more intimate and compassionate in dealing with individuals than he was with crowds.

To God, beauty is spiritual. As the one who is "perfect in beauty" dwells within us, he moves through us, reflecting real beauty in our choices, words, and behavior.

For me, this is convicting. It's easier to wear a mask on the outside than to take it off, look at the dirty rotten stuff smoldering beneath the surface, and do some housecleaning. Today we are going to take a good look at what's pretty to God and pretty to men too.

* Let's begin by reading John 13:1-17, where Jesus washes the disciples' feet. What is the example Jesus is setting for us here?

A golden nugget is embedded in this passage: "Jesus knew that the Father had put all things under his power, and that he had come from God and was returning to God" (verse 3). We are looking at a Lord who knew the authority he had, knew his value, and knew his heavenly home. But knowing his value didn't make him prideful. Instead of using his value to exalt himself, he used it for service.

* Please fill in the blanks with your name: _____
knows that the Father has granted her authority in Christ, and _____ has come from God and is returning to God.

* Please write verses 14 and 15 here:

✻ In verse 17, what does Jesus say we are blessed if we do?

As Jesus says in John 8:54, "If I glorify myself, my glory means nothing. My Father, whom you claim as your God, is the one who glorifies me." He didn't exalt himself; he exalted others. This is why Paul tells us to honor one another above ourselves (Romans 12:10). According to Hebrews 5:7, Jesus's prayers and loud cries while he was on earth were heard on high because of his "reverent submission" (Hebrews 5:7).

Whether we are married or not, we must understand that submission is simply following the example of Christ.

Please turn now to Ephesians 5 and read verses 1-2 and 22-24. Reading the introduction to this section is important so you understand the context. Submission is an overflow of love.

✻ Please draw a picture of the relationship between husband and wife. Go ahead and label the head and the body and how they relate to Christ and the church.

Have you ever disagreed with your husband so strongly that you felt like your head was going one way and your body another? I have! Yet something happens when we relinquish our own desires and follow their lead. We have peace. As long as they are not leading us into sin, submitting to their covering has a wonderful result: We obey God by honoring our husbands—even if they may be wrong—and we experience the blessing.

"Liberation through submission," my mentor Devi once told me.

I had no idea what she meant, because I felt like submitting was giving in. I was so fearful that he was making the wrong choice that I didn't want to honor his voice. Guess what? Angst and turmoil was the result.

Devi has this way of delivering a rebuke that breaks my bones in the softest, sweetest tone of voice. "The reason you don't want to submit is because you have an exalted view of your own wisdom," she told me. Ouch. True, but ouch.

Now I know the peace of headship. I don't need to wrack my brain trying to figure out if he's right; I can just follow his lead as a way to honor Christ. I can pray for him fervently, wash his feet, honor him as the king of the castle, and revere God all the while. In turn, my husband is exalted to his rightful place as leader of the home, and I experience his blessing, both private and public.

What do women really want? Peace in our homes, love from our husbands, our children to walk securely.

＊ Please pray whatever the Spirit has laid on your heart right here:

Day Two: Love Like Jesus Does

—Jewel for Your Journey—
*"You will shine among them like stars
in the sky" (Philippians 2:15).*

Honestly, some days it seems easier to shine outside the home than in it. Inside our homes, we are up close and personal with imperfect people, and the veins of our bodies pulse with deep and abiding love for them. That kind of intimacy leaves us vulnerable. We are more apt to blow it when the frustrations and worries take us over. The love runs so deep sometimes we don't even know what to do with the hurts and disappointments that come with close human relationships.

God's Word gives us a roadmap for the relationships within these walls where we live, and his principles work. I've learned the hard way how important honor and respect is for a man, and my husband has been extraordinarily patient with and forgiving of me as I've struggled to put on the new clothes of Christ—namely, honor, gentleness, self-control, and respect.

✳ Let's begin today's study with a funny verse, Proverbs 30:32-33. What does the Word call someone who exalts herself?

I love the advice here: "clap your hand over your mouth." That means *shut up!* Why? Because when we exalt our wisdom over our husband's, we stir up anger and strife. Sometimes the wisest thing we can do is be quiet.

Go ahead and read Proverbs 31:10-31. Clearly, this woman had an active life outside the home. She ran a successful enterprise, donated her time to the needy, and beautified her house with careful consideration.

✳ What do we learn about this woman in verses 10-12?

Now re-read verses 28-31. The passage begins by saying she is worth "far more" than rubies. In other words, she is priceless. Why? Because she honors her husband in the home; she brings him good and not harm all the days of his life. What is the result? Both he and their children praise her, and she receives public favor and influence.

What did Christ receive in return for his reverent submission? Public honor. Praise. Exaltation. Affirmation and approval from

God. Look back now at your picture of the head and the body, a picture of marriage. As the body honors the head, the head in turn honors the body. There is no disconnection in this picture, and since two are better than one, we have double return for our work!

Such is the story of Queen Esther, one of those radiant women of the Bible who shines from the inside out. The king searches for a truly beautiful woman and discovers the jewel of Esther. She beautifies herself with treatments galore, and when it comes time to approach the king with a big problem—the destruction of the Jews—Esther prays, fasts, waits, serves, and shows the king double honor.

As you may surmise, Esther has King Xerxes eating out of her hand. He stops the royal decree, rescues the Jews, and uses his stature to do good and speak up for the welfare of the people.

Behind every good man is a good woman, and Esther's honor transformed her husband from a drunkard into a defender of his people. Her honor made him more honorable; he became all that God designed him to be. By being humble in her home, she had tremendous influence outside of it. Esther knew what we all need to know: Honor is beautiful. Men love it, it crushes the enemy, and it saves people.

* Turn now to 1 Peter 3:1-6. How do we win our husbands' favor?

* What is beautiful in God's sight?

I was so relieved when I discovered the "gentle and quiet spirit, which is of great worth in God's sight" was not a requirement for me having a gentle and quiet *personality*. That Spirit is Christ's Spirit within us—which is undecaying, unfading, and grows stronger with time, unlike adornments, which will come and go. We draw the men in our lives to God not by our many words, but by Christ's love that lives in us.

Our love crushes the enemy. Our submission exalts God. Our respect inspires love. What if we didn't just call Jesus the light of the world, but instead we reflected his light in our homes?

* I'm going to leave this space for you to pray whatever the Spirit is putting on your heart.

My friend, I share this message with you in hopes it will bless the men in your life. Remember, you are the light of your home. Don't cover your light today. In his name, amen!

Day Three: Glory

— Jewel for Your Journey —
"The glory of the LORD *filled the temple" (2 Chronicles 7:1)*

As alluring as the world's masquerade balls are, it's time for women to speak out against the lies that lock our daughters in prison cells and speak up for what it means to be a "temple gate called Beautiful." We are not helpless to the prince of this air, luring this generation's girls to give their bodies away, exalt themselves, and succumb to the pressures of the world to be sexy, sexy, sexy as if that will make them a real star.

Instead, we must have conviction about who God is, who we are, and what on earth we are for. And we must pass that truth on to the next generation. Our bodies are holy, and his desire is to shine his light through us so that not only are we his daughters, creations, and temples, but his shining lights.

We always see who we are, what we are worth, and what our purpose is in the Word, so over the next two days, we are digging in. The only field trip we are taking this week is forward in time to the new Jerusalem, the Holy City of heaven and backward in time to the temple of the old Jerusalem. Let's go!

* We know from Revelation 22:16 that Jesus calls himself the "bright Morning Star." But let's take a look at *just how bright* he is. Read Revelation 21:1-27, John's vision of the new Jerusalem. What does this vision make you feel?

* Please write a summary of verse 3 here:

* Who is the temple in heaven (verses 22-23)?

* Who is the lamp?

If that doesn't make you want to go to heaven, I don't know what will! The city is made of gold, pure as glass; precious stones inlaid within its foundations, and its gates are made with pearls. The exact measurements of the heavenly city are reminiscent of the old temple of Jerusalem that King Solomon built in honor of his father's legacy. King David's heart dreamed of building the temple, but God passed the assignment to his son Solomon, who spared no expense and detail in both adorning it from the outside and begging God to dwell in it on the inside, as a lamp to the people.

As you read about Solomon's temple, I want you to recall the words of Paul: "We are the temple of the living God." And "your bodies are temples of the Holy Spirit" (2 Corinthians 6:16 and 1 Corinthians 6:19).

Sit back and prepare your heart to read several pages that describe the wealth, precision, dedication, glory, and power of the temple of *you*.

Because of King Solomon's humility, God granted him wisdom, wealth, riches, and honor to lead his people. Then Solomon gave orders to build a temple for the name of the Lord and a royal palace for himself.

Please read 2 Chronicles 3:1-17.

* What strikes you as interesting about the temple?

* Describe the Most Holy Place.

* You can use the space below to draw what you envision.

Second Chronicles 4 and 5 describe the lavish wealth and detail of the temple's furnishings and the placing of the Ark of the Covenant in the Most Holy Place, beneath the wings of the cherubim.

After the building of the temple was complete, the people rejoiced and celebrated, and Solomon said, "I have built a magnificent temple for you, a place for you to dwell forever" (2 Chronicles 6:2). He then dedicated the temple.

* Read 2 Chronicles 6:12-42, his prayer of dedication. What was the purpose of the temple?

* Read 2 Chronicles 7:1-3. What did God do after Solomon dedicated the temple?

Yes, God showed up, and God filled that temple with glory. Even though God cannot be contained, he filled it.

To close our study of Solomon's temple, read now what the Lord says to Solomon, in 2 Chronicles 7:11-16.

* Please write verse 16 here:

* What is God's heart for the temple for *you*?

While the world tells us our bodies are our possessions to be controlled, changed, analyzed, criticized, or flaunted, the Word tells us our bodies are his temples. I hope your reading today shows you how passionate God is about the temple. When he consecrates a temple for his Name, he is zealous about that place. You, my friend, are God's dwelling place. Your body is his holy home. May you and I treat ourselves as such, that we would be a clean and healthy and pure house for his Spirit to live, reign, and fill. It is my hope that people will be drawn to the temples of us; that we would become places where mercy reigns; that we would see our own value as pure gold; and that we would always remember, the Lamb who dwells within us is our light.

Day Four: Shine!

—Jewel for Your Journey—

"If I make you light-bearers, you don't think I'm going to hide you under a bucket, do you? I'm putting you on a light stand. Now that I've put you there on a hilltop, on a light stand—shine!" (Matthew 5:15-16 MSG).

I had a vision once about going to the temple in heaven, and the Lamb was at the center. Surrounding him were the saints—all of us—all praising him, hands raised, crying "Holy!" There were no differences between us; we were all his children, all in robes, all beautiful. It was the most overwhelming feeling of praise I have ever had in my life, and I didn't want to come "back to earth." I wanted to stay there forever.

Yet when the vision came to an end, my soul tried to stay in that place, but my body felt almost torn away. I opened my eyes, and there I was, lying on my couch in my living room. I shed a tear. Life on earth is hard and we know we're going to get to heaven someday, but sometimes I just wish it was now. Yet on the other hand, we are on this earth for a purpose—to call God's sons and daughters home.

The book of Revelation, written by the apostle John, shows us he saw *so much more*—the war for our souls, the destruction of the

Antichrist, the revealing of the Holy City, the bride of Christ, the wedding of the Lamb. He saw the end of our story. It must have made him long desperately to return to the Father.

In the beautifully adorned, fantastically designed, wonderfully made temple of heaven, Jesus is the light. We will need no sun, for he is the lamp. So it goes with us. In the temples of you and me, he is the light.

We always find out who we are and what we are here for in the reflection of who he is.

* Read John 9:5. What does Jesus say about himself?

* Made in his image, what does he say about us in Matthew 5:14-16?

I love lamps. I have some very stylish lamps in my home, and although I want to conserve electricity, I enjoy the lamps being illuminated. There is something about having a lit lamp which makes the environment feel warm and inviting. Notice that Jesus tells us we are the light of the world, and then he offers two pictures: a public light and a private light. We are "a city on a hill." People will be drawn to our light. They will see something different about us, and hopefully what they see is extraordinary love. Whether you shine your light outside the home through the Internet, the classroom, the playground, or the park, you are a public light for Christ. Serving him by loving people is the greatest thing we do.

But we cannot be a public light without also being a private light. As Jesus compares us to a lamp, he says we give light to everyone in the house. But he points out we shouldn't put our light under a "bowl." The Message version says, "You don't think I'm going to

hide you under a bucket, do you? I'm putting you on a light stand…
Shine!"

Over the last few years, our family has been under a lot of trial.
We have experienced a lot of pain. There were many days when I was
an effective "city on a hill," but came home and put a bucket over
my head. Attractive? Not!

* Do you ever find yourself "putting a bucket over your head" at
  home? How so?

* Why or why do you not choose to do that?

* What is the impact on those closest to you when you shroud
  your light?

Sometimes we look at our circumstance so much we reflect it,
and when we do that, joy is stolen from us. We are the lamps in our
homes, and we give light to everyone in the house. We simply cannot decide it's too hard and throw a blanket over our light. We have
to turn away from the circumstances and look *up*. Up, at the light.
Up! The more we look up at the Light of the World, the more we
will reflect him.

This actually takes work. It takes early morning prayers and late
night love; it takes serving when we don't feel like it and reserving
energy for our husbands and children after long, hard days when

our energy reserves feel drained. It means lighting the candle within us so those who matter most can find comfort in our peace, joy, and laughter.

Like Jesus, as long as we are in the world, we are the light of the world—in public and in private.

* Please read Philippians 2:14-16. What advice does Paul give us here?

* How do we "shine like stars in the universe"?

Here is The Message version of verses 14-15:

> "Do everything readily and cheerfully—no bickering, no second-guessing allowed! Go out into the world uncorrupted, a breath of fresh air in this squalid and polluted society. Provide people with a glimpse of good living and of the living God. Carry the light-giving Message into the night."

* What do you think it means to "carry the light-giving message into the night"?

* Please read Daniel 12:3. I have provided The Message version for you here:

"Men and women who have lived wisely and well will shine brilliantly, like the cloudless, star-strewn night skies. And those who put others on the right path to life will glow like stars forever."

✱ What makes us stars?

Satan wanted to "raise [his] throne above the stars of God," but he was brought down to the grave (Isaiah 14:13,15) by God and crushed by Jesus on the cross. Who are the stars? We are, my friend, we are. We hold out the word of life, Christ. We lead others to righteousness. We dedicate our temples to him. We invite him to fill us with his glory. We light our homes; we light our cities. It's time to shine!

Light of the world, thank you that you are all the light we need. Thank you for lighting us up from within, outside the home and inside it. Help us to be filled with your beauty and your spirit, so that we are both a city on a hill and a lamp in our homes. In Jesus's beautiful name, amen.

Day Five: Shine like Stars

—Jewel for Your Journey—
"You are the light of the world" (Matthew 5:14).

Meet with your group and watch the video "The Fourth Truth: You Are a Shining Light" at www.jenniferstrickland.net. Use the space below for notes.

Week 9 The Fifth Lie:

You Are Mastered by the Media

Day One: The Media

—Jewel for Your Journey—
"Woe to those who call evil good and good evil" (Isaiah 5:20).

Read chapter 9 and answer the following questions:
What did this chapter make you think about?

* How can you use media for good?

* How can media be bad for you?

* Please use this space to pray for your husband, children, or people in your life who could be mastered by the media.

Day Two: Test the Spirits

—Jewel for Your Journey—

"They are from the world and speak from the viewpoint of the world, and the world listens to them" (1 John 4:5).

Today we'll be taking our field trip for the week. But no need to get a babysitter—you'll be doing this one from your kitchen table! Your assignment is to talk with your family about the positive and negative influences of the media. So cook up a yummy dinner or a fun dessert, gather at the table, and do a little survey.

The Word says, "Test everything that is said. Hold on to what is good. Stay away from every kind of evil" (1 Thessalonians 5:21-22 NLT). In 1 John 4:1, we are told not to believe every spirit, but test them to see whether they are from God.

I want us to take the time to do some real thinking and talking about forms of media that are in our lives daily. So pose these questions to your family and list their answers!

* What are the good and bad things about the Internet?

* What are the good and bad things about social media?

* What are the good and bad things about video games?

* What are the good and bad things about iPhones and similar devices?

* What are the good and bad things about reality TV?

* What are the good and bad things about news media?

* What are the good and bad things about movies?

I hope that went well! I'm proud of you for taking the time to weigh the screens for good use and rightly divide what is good from what is not! I hope it also helps your children navigate that dicey collide between the values upheld by the world and the ways of God.

Light of the world, please illuminate the darkness for us so we can see it clearly and call it what it is. Show us how to use the vehicle of the media to shine the light of your glory to a world that really, really needs you. In Jesus's name, amen.

Day Three: Women in the Media

—Jewel for Your Journey—
*"Once you were full of darkness, but now you
have light from the Lord" (Ephesians 5:8).*

When it comes to the many faces of women in the media—from reality TV to movie stars to rock stars to fashion icons—what do you see as the values they uphold? I'm aware that's a broad question, and you may want to pinpoint certain television personalities or brands to focus on to answer to this question. But I want you to carefully consider your answers.

* The influence of women in the media looks like this to me:

* The values upheld by women in the media are:

* The messages women in the media are sending are:

* Women in the media whom I admire reflect these values:

Once I did a survey of women, asking them what they considered the qualities of real beauty to be. Across the board, the answers were in line with the nature of Christ. Women considered real beauty to be reflected in the qualities of patience, enduring love, forgiveness, mercy, kindness, compassion, unwavering peace, goodness, humility, service, truthfulness, faithfulness, gentleness, selflessness, and self-control—all of which reflect the Holy Spirit living inside of us.

The Spirit of Christ is the light in the temple of us. As he dwells in us, three things occur: First, his light exposes the darkness around us. Second, his light exposes the darkness within us. Third, his light shines through us so people see him living within us, and hopefully are drawn to his light.

* Please read Ephesians 5:8-16. What does it mean to expose the deeds of darkness (verse 11)?

I do not believe Christian women in the media should shy away from shining the light on the darkness. We need not glorify the deeds of darkness, but we must illuminate them. When I speak in the public schools I point out the darkness just as much as I do when I am in private schools. I let the students know what the beautiful lies of our culture are—that sex outside of marriage leads to pain, that chitchatting themselves to death on social media is fruitless, that their gifts and talents (and not their outward appearances) are the manifestation of their beauty. When we expose the darkness, people can see it for what it is and in turn, they recognize the light. When I leave the schools, my guess is most of the kids know God is my strength. By showing them the darkness, they see the light within me.

* What do you think is our responsibility as Christian women in media? (You may not be a public face, but we all have the media at our fingertips and wield it for influence.)

* Why do we need to make the most of every opportunity (verse 16)?

The light within us naturally exposes darkness. But it doesn't just expose the darkness in the world; it also illuminates the darkness within us. The cracks and crevices of our hearts where grime has grown are illuminated. Deeply ingrained sin is eventually exposed as it causes the foundation of the temple to buckle. When I first came to Christ, I was quickly convicted of my outward sins and repented. Over time, God put me on a lampstand of sorts, and I began shining a public light. Next thing I knew, he was exposing every unclean thing in my heart: bitterness, anger, resentment, self-centeredness, insubordination, rebellion, you name it—it all came into the light.

Something has to happen if we really want to walk in the light: We must be willing to allow God to expose the things we'd rather not see.

* Please read 1 John 1:5–2:17. Is there any darkness still living in you that the light is illuminating? Please share about that here, even if only you will understand its meaning.

* How are we purified from sin?

* Please use this space to agree with God that whatever he is illuminating for you is in fact sin and that you desire freedom from its weight, deliverance from its grip, and transformation in Christ.

* What is the issue John capitalizes on that will keep us walking in darkness?

* John's entire letter is about walking in the light, being filled by the Spirit, not continuing to sin, and loving one's brother. Please read 1 John 3:7-24. What does he tell us about love?

* Let's close this day with a vision of what love looks like, in 1 Corinthians 13:1-7. How are these the traits of a beautiful woman?

The light living in us really comes down to one word: love. As women who wield influence—either on Facebook or in classrooms or in the home—we have an opportunity to be the light of the world. We can dedicate our temples to him; we can ask him to fill us with his glory. We can choose to let him illuminate the darkness within us so we can be clean of it, and we can use his light to shine in the darkest parts of the earth. Finally, we can make sure that he shines within us, from the inside out, the light of love, the traits of the truly beautiful woman. Maybe, just maybe, together we can redefine women's beauty and value for a world that is in dire need of a new definition.

Day Four: The Temple Gate

—Jewel for Your Journey—
*"We cannot help speaking about what we
have seen and heard" (Acts 4:20).*

I'm excited for this day of study because we are actually going to hang out in front of the temple gate called Beautiful. This is one of my very favorite stories in Scripture and I hope you will be as excited and amazed by its revelations as I am. Let's pray!

Light of the World, you bask in unapproachable light. You are the lamp at the center of heaven and earth. You are the light inside of us. When it comes to the media, how do we shine your light? Show us what it means to be a temple gate called Beautiful today. We love you and praise you. In your name, Jesus, amen.

* Please read Acts 3:1-10, one of the first stories in the book of Acts, which records the acts of the apostles after Jesus's death, burial, resurrection, and ascension into heaven. In verse, 4, what does Peter do?

Peter wanted to go face-to-face. He locked eyes with the beggar. He wasn't afraid to look straight into the face of suffering and speak truth into it.

* What happened to the man? What was the response of the people?

* Read on through verse 16. What does Peter use this opportunity to say?

* Continue reading through Acts 4:4. It is clear Peter understands the history of the prophets. How does this make him an effective witness?

* What is the reaction of the priests and religious leaders?

* Read Acts 4:5-31. Not only was this a countercultural message in their day, but it still is in ours. In what way does this message boldly stand in the way of the vast majority of messages of the media?

* How is the prophecy quoted in verse 26 still true today?

We can either choose to rush by the beggars of the world or stop and look at one. We can either choose to avoid the face of suffering or boldly look it square in the eye. When we are challenged on our beliefs, we can either choose to water down the gospel and shy away from its central truth (see verse 12, which you wrote above) or we choose to please God over man. These choices are up to us.

Ladies, we are temple gates called Beautiful. There are beggars all around us. Accusers too. Yet the "one who is in you is greater than the one who is in the world" (1 John 4:4). Believe it and live it! Together, we are made for more! More power, more influence, more light, more truth, more healing, and more salvation. Watch out, world, here we come—bolder than ever.

In the name that is above every name, I pray a spirit of boldness will fill our hearts and that we will make the most of every opportunity to go face-to-face with people who need you, to love the hurting, to touch the suffering, to speak the gospel message, to your glory and for your honor and praise forever and ever. Amen.

Day Five: Voices of the Media

—Jewel for Your Journey—
"Enable your servants to speak your word with great boldness" (Acts 4:29).

Meet with your group and watch the video "The Fifth Lie: You Are Mastered by the Media" at www.jenniferstrickland.net. Use the space below for notes.

Week 10   The Fifth Truth:

You Are a Chosen Ambassador

Day One: My Food

—Jewel for Your Journey—
*"'My food,' said Jesus, 'is to do the will of him who
sent me and to finish his work'" (John 4:34).*

Read chapter 10 and use the space below to write your reactions to this last chapter.

Before we embark on this final week together, I just want to say thank you for taking this journey with me. Thank you for taking a chance on me, for trusting me to hold up these five mirrors of the world and five mirrors of the Word. I am honored and blessed to have been your guide. It's so interesting how the world's mirrors shift and change, but God's mirror is crystal clear. The world's mirrors will pass away, but the Word of our God will last forever.

I am so grateful for the Word. Maybe because for the first 23 years of my life, I didn't have it. There were a few Bibles around me growing up, passed down from believing relatives but gathering dust on shelves. I didn't look closely at the living words on the page until the world's mirrors had so confounded me I was desperate for truth.

The believers I met while I was modeling in Europe were living stars. They held out the Word of life to a forlorn, forsaken, and foreign girl. Standing beneath the gazebo in the park of the River Isar in Munich, Germany, these ambassadors had the boldness to look one beggar in the face, and that beggar was me. Handing out New Testaments from a cardboard box, playing music beneath the arched colonnade that adorned the gazebo, they must have believed his Word would not return void. When they handed one girl the Word, they bet right. These strangers knew me for a very short time, in which they explained the gospel message to me, invited me to their church, and rejoiced when I accepted Christ. Through this single face-to-face encounter in the park, more girls have been touched than they could have ever dreamed.

This week we will study your fifth identity in Christ, the ambassador. And your last field trip, which can happen any day this week, will be to do something you have possibly never done: As you are going on your way, running your errands, getting your groceries, or doing whatever it is you do, I want you to listen for the Spirit's voice. Ask him, "Who's the beggar?" When you sense that person is before you, look him or her in the face, into the eyes, and offer the one thing that heals the lame man inside of all of us: Jesus.

You may be so bold as to hand out Bibles in a park; you may be so quiet as to look into your neighbor's eyes. You may never know what will come of your investment. Yet it really isn't ours to know, is it? His ways are not the world's ways. We really don't need recognition when we are doing what we were created to do: reflect his image, his heart, his faith, and his love.

"My food," Jesus said, "is to do the will of the one who sent me and to finish his work." There is nothing more fulfilling than doing the work of God. And he's not finished working. Jesus told us we would do even greater things than he (John 14:12). Hard to imagine, but true. Together, you and I are living stones, precious jewels, casting his light wherever we go.

Day Two: The Most High

—Jewel for Your Journey—
*"The holy people of the Most High will receive
the kingdom and will possess it forever—
yes, for ever and ever" (Daniel 7:18).*

I've been saying it all along: We see who we are in the reflection of who he is. Yet with this fifth and final mirror of our journey together, not only do we see our identity and purpose, but we also see our power. Did you know the demons tremble at the name of the Most High? Did you know they are terrified by his Son? Did you know we are representatives of an eternal kingdom that will never perish, spoil, or fade, and that we have the power of the Most High God within us?

If you don't already have some guts, over the next three days, we are going to get some. We are going to take hold of the formidable force inside of us and the powers or darkness will be running for cover.

Let's pray.

Oh Sovereign God, your name is above every other name; your dominion will never end. You are our Father, our Creator, the Lord of lords and King of kings, and you are the Most High God. Your power and might is greater than any force upon the earth, and we submit ourselves to your authority today and rest in the shadow of your wings. Show us who you are, God, and help us see our reflection in the mirror of your face, the most Ancient of Days. In Jesus's precious blood we pray, amen.

* Please turn to Psalm 83:18. What is God called here?

* Flip over to Psalm 97 and read verses 1-9. In verses 2-5, how is
  the Lord's power manifested?

* Verse 7 tells us that all who worship images are

  _____.

* In verse 9, the Most High is exalted far above

  _____.

We are now going to turn to the book of Daniel to read his amazing vision of God and the destruction of the enemy through Christ.
In the succeeding passage, Daniel describes a vision in which he saw
four great beasts. The fourth one was different from all the rest; it
devoured and crushed its victims, trampling them underfoot. This
beast, as we will see soon in Revelation, represents Babylon, the evil
city that rejoiced in adultery to God. This city exalted itself above
the Most High, just like Satan, and was filled with pomposity.

* Begin by reading Daniel 7:1 to understand our context, and then
  skip down to the description of the fourth beast in verses 7-8.
  How many horns did this beast have?

  _____.

* What kind of words was the mouth speaking?

Now, continue reading Daniel's amazing vision of God in verses
9-10. This is remarkably similar to the description of God in Psalm
50:2-3: "From Zion, perfect in beauty, God shines forth. Our God
comes and will not be silent; a fire devours before him, and around
him a tempest rages."

So many people are under the mistaken impression that God is the antithesis of Satan. It's nowhere near true. Satan was a created being. When he tried to exalt himself above the Most High, God sent him squealing out of heaven with no ticket back in. Although Satan is the only other created being called "perfect in beauty," he destroyed his beauty due to pride.

God's perfect beauty, however, reigns supreme; his throne rides on flaming fire. There is not a created being in all the world that can hold a candle to the Most High.

We will return to Daniel's vision later. For now, we will turn back to Isaiah 14. As you read, understand that the cities of Babylon and Assyria, referenced here, are symbolic of souls sick with pride. The king in this passage may represent Satan, or Nebuchadnezzar, the prideful king of Babylon, who was given positional greatness just like the enemy. But when Nebuchadnezzar's heart grew proud, God reduced him to naught. Whether these verses are about the devil or a king, or both, what you see is a Most High God who will not be trumped. You see a supreme authority who crushes kings in their wickedness and destroys the evil one forever.

❋ Read Isaiah 14:13-15. Who did Satan want to make himself like?

As we know from Ezekiel 28:17-18, his heart became proud on account of his beauty and he corrupted his wisdom because of his splendor. So God threw him to the earth; making a spectacle of him before kings…he made a fire come out of him and it consumed him, and God "reduced [him] to ashes on the ground in the sight of all who were watching."

What was the spectacle in which God reduced the enemy to ashes? The cross. In the words of Colossians 2:15, "having disarmed

the powers and authorities, he made a public spectacle of them, tri-
umphing over them by the cross."

* Read Isaiah 14:16-27. What does God do to the evil, prideful
  king for his pomposity?

* How is the king's fate in verses 21-22 similar to that of the enemy?

One thing about Satan we must remember is that he is *not*
invited back. He is "not to rise," he is "cut off" forever. I love verses
23-24: "I will sweep her with the broom of destruction...Surely, as I
have planned, so it will be, and as I have purposed, so it will happen."

Certainly "the plan determined for the whole world" was to
deliver us from the yoke of the enemy, to release us from his burden,
and to restore us as free children. Sometimes what we don't realize
is that when Jesus breathed his last, saying "It is finished," he really
meant it (John 19:30)!

Let's read about the fall of Babylon in the book of Revelation,
which represents not only that adulterous city, but also Rome,
where the blood of so many Christians was shed. Ultimately this
passage refers to the greatest adulterer of all, the beast of hell, Satan.

My sister and friend, sometimes I am overwhelmed by subjects
like sex trafficking, human slavery, prostitution, alcoholism, and the
murder of the innocent. I get angry that people rejoice in the tor-
ture of Christians, the mutilation of children, and the rape of young
girls. It feels like these sins are insurmountable, like we cannot conquer them. But God can. Watch what God does to destroy the great
prostitute who sets herself up against the honor of the Most High.

Read Revelation 17:1-6. Here we see that the beast is called "the great prostitute," and that the people are "intoxicated with the wine of her adulteries."

Read Revelation 18:1-10. Notice this beast is destroyed in one day, in one hour (verse 10).

* Turn back now to our final words for this day, in Daniel 7:11-14. What happened to the beast? What was he thrown into?

* Who showed up as soon as the beast was destroyed?

* Continue reading Daniel's interpretation of the dream in verses 15-22. This fourth beast was waging war against the saints and defeating them, until what happened?

* Who won the war? Summarize verse 22:

We win, friend. We are the saints of the Most High, and we win. Poor Daniel—verse 28 says he was extremely troubled by what he saw and his face turned pale. I bet it did! I bet that man was absolutely overwhelmed with awe for that Ancient of Days who pronounced judgment on the beast and finished him off forever.

The amazing thing is, the Most High hands us the keys to the kingdom, to possess it for eternity, "yes, for ever and ever" (Daniel 7:18). He tells us that three times in the book of Daniel alone, and many other times in Scripture. I think he wants to remind us who we belong to and what our inheritance is—the kingdom, forever and ever, amen.

Sovereign God, please don't let us ever forget that when you crushed your Son on the cross, you threw the enemy into the lake of fire. His dominion on this earth is over. Your dominion never ends. As life gets hard and the world's systems stand to overwhelm us, please don't let us forget who you are—the Most High—and whose we are—your saints. Thank you that you've already fought for us, we've already won, and you sided on our behalf. Just God, proclaim justice on the earth. In Jesus's name, amen.

Day Three: Chosen

—Jewel for Your Journey—

"We are therefore Christ's ambassadors, as though God were making his appeal through us" (2 Corinthians 5:20).

We left off yesterday at the doom of the enemy. By one sacrifice, in one day, we were reconciled to God and called sons and daughters of the Most High. Today we are going to look at Mary Magdalene, Christ's chosen ambassador.

* Read Luke 8:1-3. What do we know about Mary Magdalene's life?

You don't really think twelve guys and a bunch of others could travel around for years without women to take care of them, do you? No way! The women were there the whole time! How else would they eat, for goodness sakes?

In all sincerity, I don't think Mary could have done anything else with her life. Jesus put her in her right mind. He healed her infirmities and gave her purpose and a destiny, to carry the keys of the kingdom. What greater purpose could she have than that?

* But when Jesus died, so did her hopes. Her heart connection to him was so intimate, so tender, that she couldn't even tear herself away from the tomb. Read John 20:1-13. When the disciples went back to their homes, what did Mary Magdalene do?

* What did the angels ask her?

* Why do you think Mary was crying?

* Please read the rest of this account in verses 14-18. How do you think she felt when she heard her name?

* What does Jesus tell Mary to do?

* Where was he headed?

Mary was one special lady. She was the first one to announce Christ's resurrection; he entrusted her with much.

* Please read the account of Jesus's visitation to the disciples behind locked doors in Luke 24:36-53. What does he call them in verse 48?

* What does he tell them they will be clothed with?

The gift he promised would give them power was the Holy Spirit, and when the Holy Spirit came in the book of Acts, the people were empowered to do all kinds of glorious things. They would prophesy, see visions, heal the crippled, cast out demons, and see wonders in heaven and signs on the earth below.

So those of us too who have been baptized by the Holy Spirit are empowered to do all kinds of glorious things! So we too are called his witnesses. So we too are clothed with power from on high. So this destiny was not only for them; he said he would pour out his Spirit on *all* of us.

* Please read your identity in Isaiah 43:10-13. Who are we? What does he want us to know and understand?

Christ was God's chosen instrument; we are Christ's chosen instruments. Jesus said that he "chose us out of the world" to be his witnesses (John 15:19). He chose Mary, he chose Peter, he chose Paul, he chose me, he chose you!

Mary was the first ambassador, yet there were many more after her. You and I are included in that number.

Ladies, God is appealing to the world through us. We even have the media at our fingertips! How powerful is the light you can shine! What an impact we can make! What a voice we can cry! What truth we can share!

We are his chosen representatives, his witnesses, empowered from on high, and he's not interested in leaving the world as it is. Through us, he wants to reconcile the world to himself. In the words of Paul, "That's why I work and struggle so hard, depending on Christ's mighty power that works within me" (Colossians 1:29 NLT).

* In what way can you serve as a witness?

Day Four: When Trouble Comes

— Jewel for Your Journey —

"You, dear children, are from God and have overcome them, because the one who is in you is greater than the one who is in the world" (1 John 4:4).

In the words of Jesus, "In this world you will have trouble. But take heart! I have overcome the world" (John 16:33). My friend, trouble is brewing. This world is full of trouble, and we each have our fair share of it.

If you are living as a daughter of the Most High, you will not only have trouble, but you will also have potent spiritual opposition. You are a threat to the evil one and he hates you. Why? Because you get to go to heaven, and he's stuck in hell forever. He wants you to eat ashes like him. But what did Jesus come to do?

* Please begin today's study in Isaiah 61:1-3. Fill in the blanks:

God sent Jesus to proclaim _____.

To bind up the _____.

To proclaim _____.

To release the _____.

To comfort all who _____.

To provide for those who _____.

To bestow on them a _____ instead of ashes.

The oil of _____ instead of
_____.

And a garment of _____ instead of a spirit of _____.

That's right, my friend. In exchange for ashes, Jesus gave us a crown of beauty. In exchange for despair, he gave us a garment of praise. The crown he gives us and the dress we wear symbolize our beauty, value, and authority over the darkness.

I believe in wearing the crown well, but I must admit, there have been times mine has been knocked aside and fallen off and gotten chipped. There have been times when I've been faced with so much trouble, I've let despair creep in and take over my face.

That's exactly what the enemy wants: us eating our ashes, covered with despair. But the trials in our lives are meant to perfect us in Christ. We must commit to take our trials and let those fiery furnaces produce in us the nature of our Lord. And we must realize, as Jesus did, that "our struggle is not against flesh and blood, but against the rulers, against the authorities, against the powers of this dark world and against the spiritual forces of evil in the heavenly realms" (Ephesians 6:12).

* Let's read Paul's advice on how to stand strong in Ephesians 6:10-20. What advice jumps out at you here, as this ambassador advises us on how to stand firm?

The biggest thing that stands out to me right now is *prayer*. Prayer and praise are our greatest weapons against the enemy. We cannot be blind to the fact that the times are dark and getting darker. We can't shrink back. We can't be weak. We must be strong! We've got to put on the belt of truth and the breastplate of righteousness. We absolutely must know how to wield our swords and our feet must always be ready with the gospel of peace.

* Please read Isaiah 52:1-10. What does God say to the Daughter of Zion? How is she to clothe herself? Is she to sit back, or sit enthroned?

All day long the enemy is going to mock you. And all day long God's name is blasphemed, just as Isaiah writes. But you and I, my friend, are made for more. We are the freed daughters of Zion, and we will not be taken down.

* What does verse 7 tell you is beautiful to God?

You are beautiful in God's eyes. You are the deliverer of the good news. You are his daughter, his creation, his vessel, his light, his ambassador. And he will take care of you. When life gets hard—and it will—rest between his wings. Rest in Jesus. Enter the Most Holy

Place and wait there for him to speak to you or comfort you or bless you with peace. He is your refuge and your fortress.

* Please read Psalm 91. Where will you find refuge (verse 4)?

* If you make him your refuge, what does he promise you?

* Please record verses 14-15 here.

* Please read Jesus's predictions on what God's witnesses would have to face in Mark 13:5-13. Have you ever felt deceived? Betrayed? Abandoned? Forsaken? Denied? Accused? Hated? Boy, I have. Who does he say will speak through us at times like this (verse 11)?

* What is Jesus's advice to us in verse 13?

As Paul said, we are to rejoice in our sufferings because "suffering produces perseverance; perseverance, character; and character, hope" (Romans 5:3-4). We are going to suffer. That's the bottom line. But it's up to us to allow our trials to form in us the nature of Christ.

✳ Turn to James 1:2-4 and summarize it here. What does perseverance produce in us?

There was a time in my life not long ago when I seemed to wake up every morning saying the same thing to the Lord: "Make me more like you, Lord. Make me more like you." I would repeat this over and over again.

Then, for two and a half years, I suffered. I gave my heart and was rejected; I tried to clean my temple and was mocked and accused. I spoke up for truth and was accused of being evil. I spoke against the enemy, and was betrayed by my own kin. In the words of Peter, "Don't be surprised at the painful trial you are suffering, as though something strange were happening to you."

✳ Please read 1 Peter 4:12-19. When we suffer, what are we to do (verse 19)?

During my season of suffering, I kept getting calls to share my testimony in the churches. I felt like a dying woman on the outside, but Christ in me kept rising up and speaking. As our jewel for today's journey says, "the one who is in you is greater than the one who is in the world." My friend, no matter what you face, commit yourself to your faithful Creator and continue to do good. This is beautiful to him.

* How can you "continue to do good" during whatever trial you are facing?

Let's pray.

Dear Most High God, we are your daughters, your creations, your temples, your lights, and your ambassadors. Trouble surrounds us. Protect us. Help us to remember where to run when we need you—the tomb, the garden, the resting place between the wings of the Most High. Help us to remember you are our refuge, our hiding place from the storm and the rain, our faithful Father and our deliverer. Be with us as you promise you will be. In Jesus's name, amen.

Day Five: More Than Conquerors

—Jewel for Your Journey—

"They triumphed over him by the blood of the Lamb and by the word of their testimony" (Revelation 12:11).

Meet with your group and watch the video "The Fifth Truth: You Are His Chosen Ambassador" at www.jenniferstrickland.net. On this final day together, there are a few verses and discussion questions I'd like you to look at as a group. Take turns reading out loud and let the Holy Spirit guide your discussion.

* Turn now to Revelation 12:10-11, two short verses that say it all. According to these verses, how do we overcome the evil one?

We all have a story, a testimony of how God has showed himself faithful to us. And we all have the blood of the Lamb. These two jewels, when combined, make the precious foundation on which to build our lives. This whole journey, we have cherished the precious stones of our pathway—the foundational words of life that we can build upon.

Jesus himself was called a living Stone—rejected by men but chosen by God and precious to him. And he too calls us living stones.

* Please turn to 1 Peter 2:4-6. If we trust in him, what will we never be put to?

* Read on in verses 9-12. Who are we? (verse 9) What is our purpose?

* What are we to declare?

* How do we defeat the accusations of others?

As Paul writes in Romans 12:21, "Do not be overcome by evil, but overcome evil with good." The world has so much evil in it, and studying the influence of the media can be frightening. Evil can come into our homes via the Internet, TV, our phones, you name it. Evil is everywhere. But we are not to be overcome by it; instead, we are to stand firm and overcome evil with good.

If you have a voice, use it for good. A gift? Use it for good. A talent? Use it for good. We are representatives of a good God who brings Good News; don't forget it. And when trials come, remember this: By the blood of the Lamb and the word of our testimony, we shall overcome. This is true even of the martyrs, who spoke the truth in Jesus's name and stood firm even unto their death.

As ambassadors of the Most High, we must speak in boldness—the blood of the Lamb and the word of our testimony. We must never stop speaking it. Remember, the demons are terrified of the Most High. They shudder at his name. Simply proclaiming the blood of Jesus over any environment has the power to make the demons run for fear. In Mark 5:1-13, the demons themselves called Jesus the "Son of the Most High God." They know who he is!

And with a word, Jesus cast out the demons from a man who was crying in torment day and night, cutting himself with stones. So it is with so many children of this generation—crying out and wounding themselves, unable to be controlled, unable to control themselves. Yet there is a power higher than the power that binds their souls in torment; it is the power of the Most High.

Sometimes we are so confounded by the issues facing the girls of our generation, and we feel helpless to them. We are not helpless. The only one who is helpless is Satan himself; neither he nor any of his principalities have a way back to the Holy of Holies. But we do. Every child on earth has a way back. The cross is our way; Jesus is our gate.

Jesus said, "All authority in heaven and on earth has been given to me. Therefore go and make disciples of all nations, baptizing them in the name of the Father and of the Son and of the Holy Spirit, and teaching them to obey everything I have commanded you. And surely I am with you always, to the very end of the age" (Matthew 28:18-20).

Chosen one: Go. Make. Tell. Baptize. Teach. Love. Preach. Forgive. Believe. Empower. He is with you; he will never leave you.

We only have two jewels left on our journey. I will miss you! Please read Isaiah 54:10-17.

* What does God say he's going to build us into?

* What does God say to us in the face of tyranny and terror?

* What is the heritage of the servants of the Lord?

As he tells us in Revelation 21:7, he who overcomes will inherit the right to walk with him forever—as a man talks with his friend, so we will walk with God in the cool of the day. He will be with us. He will be our God, and we will be his bride.

Read Revelation 22:12-13. He is the Alpha and the Omega, the First and the Last, the Beginning and the End. And he is coming soon!

I can't wait to see his face. He will wipe every tear from our eyes.

He will carry us on his shoulders. And I can't wait to see heaven—there you will be, a living stone—his beloved, precious, beautiful, radiant, and chosen. Evermore.

Love,

Jen

•

Your eyes will see the king in his beauty
and a land that stretches afar.

ISAIAH 33:17